RESEARCH METHODOLOGY

RESEARCH METHODOLOGY

Dr. N. THANULINGOM
Formerly Senior Professor and Head
Department of Commerce,
Madurai Kamaraj University,
Madurai

Himalaya Publishing House
ISO 9001:2015 CERTIFIED

Millennium Edition	:	2000
Reprint	:	2001, 2003, 2005, 2007, 2009
Second Revised Edition	:	2011
Reprint	:	2019, 2021
Reprint	:	**2025**

Published by : Mrs. Meena Pandey
for **HIMALAYA PUBLISHING HOUSE PVT. LTD.,**
"Ramdoot", Dr. Bhalerao Marg, Girgaon, Mumbai - 400 004.
Phone: 022-23860170, 23863863; **Fax:** 022-23877178
E-mail: himpub@bharatmail.co.in; **Website:** www.himpub.com

Branch Offices :

New Delhi : "Pooja Apartments", 4-B, Murari Lal Street, Ansari Road, Darya Ganj, New Delhi - 110 002.
Phone: 011-23270392, 23278631; Fax: 011-23256286

Nagpur : Kundanlal Chandak Industrial Estate, Ghat Road, Nagpur - 440 018. Mobile: 09325409992, 09325908881

Bengaluru : Plot No. 91-33, 2nd Main Road, Seshadripuram, Behind Nataraja Theatre, Bengaluru - 560 020.
Phone: 080-41138821; Mobile: 09379847017, 09379847005

Hyderabad : No. 3-4-184, Lingampally, Besides Raghavendra Swamy Matham, Kachiguda, Hyderabad - 500 027.
Phone: 040-27560041, 27550139

Chennai : No. 34/44, Motilal Street, T. Nagar, Chennai - 600 017.
Mobile: 09380460419

Pune : "Laksha" Apartment, First Floor, No. 527, Mehunpura, Shaniwarpeth (Near Prabhat Theatre), Pune - 411 030.
Phone: 020-24496323, 24496333; Mobile: 09370579333

Cuttack : Plot No 5F-755/4, Sector-9, CDA Markat Nagar, Cuttack - 753 014, Odisha. Mobile: 09338746007

Kolkata : 3, S.M. Bose Road, Near Gate No. 5, Agarpara Railway Station, North 24 Parganas, West Bengal - 700109.
Mobile: 09674536325

Printed at : M/s. Sri Sai Art Printer, Hyderabad. On behalf of HPH.)P

PREFACE

Research Methodology is that common language — the science of collecting, codifying and presenting facts in such a way that it leads to unearthing some truths or angles of reality. This book aims at a lucid exposition of the various concepts and techniques used in research. It is intended as a textbooks primarily for research scholars pursuing research leading to their M.Phil. and Ph.D. degrees, Post-Graduate students, Practioners and some Under Graduate students.

I could not have written this book without the moral support of my students who deck high positions in Universities, Colleges and Business institutions. It would be difficult for me to acknowledge my indebtedness to all such people individually. I take this opportunity to thank my students, friends and well wishers for their encouragement and support.

It is my bounden duty to acknowledge the management and staff of Himalaya Publishing House for bring out this book in the present shape and my special thanks to Mr. K. Sivadasan of Himalaya Publishing House, who stood by me in this effort and whose confidence in the work never wavered.

I have gained from the clarity of thinking and the depth of knowledge of my teachers, which prompted me to bring out this book. I dedicate this book to them.

Dr. N. THANULINGOM

CONTENTS

CHAPTER ONE

NATURE OF RESEARCH

1. *Research — An Introduction*
2. *Classification of Research*
3. *Business Research — Its Nature and Scope*
4. *Benefits of Research.*

1. RESEARCH — AN INTRODUCTION

One of the basic desires of man is to know of things around him. He wants to understand fully the things of the world. No wonder does a man wish to acquire knowledge by enquiry. He asks so many questions such as why? How? When? of a thing. He is desirous of finding answers to such questions.

Moreover, in day-to-day life, man confronts numerous problems, for which he wants to find immediate solution.

Thus, man asks questions and finds answers. His efforts to find answers is the outcome of a man's thirst for knowledge. This prompts him to find solutions to problems and urges him to do something better or more efficiently.

Such questions and problems crop up from the observation of an event or series of events. Sir Isaac Newton propounded the Law of Gravitation by observing the apples falling from the apple tree. He started asking the questions "why do apples regularly fall to the ground instead of floating off into space?"[1] This enquiry led to the discovery of the Law of Gravitation.

1.1 WAYS OF GAINING KNOWLEDGE

Aristotle, the Greek philosopher found out a method of gaining knowledge called syllogism or deductive logic. A complete argument containing reasons and a conclusion is called a syllogism. In every syllogism there are two parts: One part is reason and the other one is conclusion. In Logic, a special name is given to reasons and they are called premises. The syllogism therefore consists of the premises and the conclusion. The premises are drawn from direct observation of nature. The following example illustrates the method.

(i) All men are mortal – Major premise.

(ii) Mr. Wisdom is a man – Minor premise.

(iii) Hence Mr. Wisdom is mortal – Conclusion.

If the premises are false, we shall get a false conclusion. Take the following argument.

An object which is heavier than water will float on it.

The stone is heavier than water.

Therefore, the stone will float on water. It is false to state that an object which is heavier than water will float on it. Even if one of the premises is false, the conclusion will also be false.

The process of reasoning from particular to a whole group of ideas called induction was developed by Francis Bacon as an alternative to deductive logic. For example :

Mr. Honesty is intelligent,

Mr. Honesty was born on Monday,

So all men born on Monday are intelligent.

The inductive method of reasoning consists of studying many individual cases in order to formulate a generalised conclusion. This procedure is followed in most research projects. The four conditions essential to the satisfactory induction are as follows :

(i) Observations must be correctly performed and recorded.

(ii) Observations must cover representative cases.

(iii) Observations must cover a sufficient number of cases.

(iv) Conclusions must be confirmed by statements that are fully substantiated by the findings.

Charles Pierce, the American philosopher has suggested four general ways of gaining knowledge :

(i) Method of tenacity — We hold something true because we have believed it for a long time. Old people's tales are included in this method.

(ii) Method of authority — Some persons like teachers and religious leaders holding positions of authority make statements, which are accepted by us.

(iii) Method of intuition — Certain ideas found reasonable are accepted by us. Men easily guess that women are soft spoken.

(iv) Method of science — Ideas are accepted only after they have been meticulously tested.[2]

The first three methods are called unscientific methods, since they stress on acquiring knowledge through chance, trial and error and generalising from experiences. The fourth method is called scientific method. The widely used nomenclature for the scientific method is Research.

1.2 RESEARCH

The word 'Research' is derived from the French word, 'Researcher' meaning 'to search back'. A man in his social, economic, educational, political and business life faces many problems.

1.2.1 DEFINITION OF RESEARCH

Some of the important definitions of research by well known authors are given below :

Fred Kerlinger: "Research is an organised enquiry designed and carried out to provide information for solving a problem."[3]

Francis Rummel: "Research is a careful inquiry or examination to discover new information or relationships and to expand and to verify existing knowledge."[4]

Robert Ross: "Research is essentially an investigation, a recording and analysis of evidence for the purpose of gaining knowledge."[5]

The purpose of research is gaining knowledge, which will be used for solving problems (applied research) or for satisfying one's thirst for knowledge (pure research). Before undertaking research, a researcher presents a crystal clear view of his goal. The goals of research may be discovering new facts, establishment of new relationship, creation of new concepts, verification of existing concepts, finding solution to a problem or satisfying one's desire to know.

In order to achieve the goal of the researcher, evidence has to be collected. The evidence may be empirical (field study) or printed material or both. The main methods ensuring the gathering of field study evidence are interview, questionnaire, and observation. Printed sources considered to be basic are books, pamphlets, periodicals, government documents, master's theses and doctoral dissertations. Recent years have witnessed the emergence of new kinds of sources of evidence. They are microfilms, micrographs, microfiches, tapes, slides, film strips, video tapes and other devices. Nowadays many kinds of visual materials such as photographs, drawings, flow charts, geographical maps, map graphs, tables, graphs and the like, also have enhanced true potentiality of necessary evidence.

The evidence has to be collected through investigation. The investigation must be exhaustive and accurate. No dishonesty should creep into the investigation. Before investigation, it is imperative that a subject should be chosen, a problem should be formed and a hypothesis should be framed. Then alone should the collection of evidence be done, material prudently organised and finally conclusions be drawn and the thesis written.

While investigating, the collected evidence, must be recorded. After its collection, the evidence, should be judiciously processed and presented in the usable form. Afterwards, the evidence must be synthesized and the report prepared. The report may be a term paper, a library paper, a long paper, a documented paper, a master's thesis, a creative thesis, a scientific thesis or a doctoral dissertation.

According to Professor Glifford Moody, research is a method of discovering truth, through critical thinking. He says "Research comprises defining and redefining problems; formulating hypothesis or suggested solutions; collecting, organising and evaluating data; making deductions and making conclusions; and at last, carefully testing the conclusions to determine whether they fit the formulated hypothesis."[6] This definition emphasises three types of research : Firstly, the discovery of facts as in social surveys, secondly the analysis and interpretation of secondary data already collected and finally building up of theory based on primary and secondary data and sometimes on the basis of pure reasoning. In theory building, thinking of the highest order is quite essential; whereas in the survey variety, it is least important.

Research or Scientific method is nothing but a systematic process and it is composed of several prescribed steps:

(i) Identification of a research question.

(ii) Formulation of hypothesis or predictions about the question in advance of the study.

(iii) Design of the study to test the hypothesis.

(iv) Observation of variables.

(v) Examination of relationships between the variables observed and

(vi) Drawing conclusions about the research questions based on observed relationship.

This process is a continuous cycle in which the conclusions reached on the basis of one study may lead to a reformulation of original hypothesis or to new research questions for future investigation. Again, the procedure followed by a researcher and the conclusions reached can be independently verified or evaluated by other researchers.

1.2.2 NORMS GUIDING THE RESEARCHER

A number of norms, which commonly guide the researcher in the pursuit of knowledge, have been identified.

(i) Faith in rationality.

(ii) Emotional neutrality towards ideas and research findings.

(iii) Belief in the universal right of all people to claims of discovery and possession of knowledge.

(iv) Individualism or the unwillingness to be swayed by the majority.

(v) Belief in the larger interest of the community.

(vi) Uninterestedness in personal prestige or self-interest.

(vii) Impartiality in the production and evaluation of new knowledge.

(viii) Suspension of judgement in the absence of conclusive evidence.

(ix) Absence of bias in evaluating the work of others.

(x) Belief that the production of new knowledge by research is the most important of all activities.

(xi) Resistance to control over scientific investigation.

1.2.3 QUALITIES OF A RESEARCHER

The researcher should be a man of science in the true sense of the word. He is firmly committed to the 'articles of faith' of the scientific method. Sir Michael Foster identified the following three qualities, in a scientist. These qualities are also expected of a researcher.

The researcher should have an alert mind. Nature provides inexhaustible sources of information. The researcher should be keenly receptive to the gestures of nature and should be in readiness to gather game of knowledge.

The researcher needs to be induced with the quality of moral courage. The prosecution of research is not a bed of roses but it is a path beset with the hardship of time and again the researcher may feel defeated and lost in wilderness. Very often the encouragement he gets from the subjects of his study may help him to keep his interest unflagging. Difficulties caused by lack of response from the subjects may waste his endeavour.

The researcher should be truthful. Truth should be his watchword. Truthfulness will ensure accuracy of observation and precision of statement. Truthlessness may distort the correct view of men.

1.3 SOCIAL RESEARCH

Like physical, biological and technological research, social research commands equal importance as a major field of research. Social research includes social sciences, humanities and languages.

Social research incorporates man and his institutions. It is largely empirical and it does not believe in arm-chair research. Social research is bound to be inter-disciplinary as the social phenomena are not isolated.

Rummel : "Social Research is devoted to a study of mankind in his social environment and is concerned with improving his understanding of social orders, groups, institutions and ethics."[8]

The relevance of social research is far greater in developing countries like India, Bangladesh etc. which are confronted with complex socio-economic problems like poverty, unemployment, underemployment, illiteracy and the like. The important features of social research are the following:

(i) Social research provides the basic data for social planning.

(ii) The first-hand knowledge about the organisation and working of the society and its institutions is obtained from the social research.

(iii) Social research promotes social cohesion and better understanding in the society.

(iv) Social research enables the researcher to have intimate knowledge of the society and such knowledge guides social growth on proper lines.

(v) A large portion of legislation and reformative measures owe their origin to the reports of social surveys.

1.4 BUSINESS RESEARCH

Research in all aspects of business is becoming increasingly important in the major countries of the world. It is a method of obtaining and evaluating data for the decision process. Business research is both basic and applied. Basic research is carried on for the purpose of extending the frontiers of knowledge. Applied research is problem-oriented in that the research is carried on to solve a specific problem about which a decision must be reached. For example financial research may be carried on for the purpose of making a decision among alternative investment opportunities or among alternative sources of capital funds. One of the important characteristics of business research is that the results are to be decision-oriented.

The experimental, historical and statistical methods are the three general methods followed in research investigation. They are also followed in business research.

A wide range of subject areas comes within the purview of research in business areas. A substantial amount of research has been done in human relations management such as studies of morale, employee opinion and attitudes, absenteeism, internal communication, the management of people and interpersonal transaction processes.

2. CLASSIFICATION OF RESEARCH

Great difficulties beset the classification of research into some universally accepted categories. The distinctions among the different types of studies are not clear-cut; nevertheless the need for formulating appropriate research designs, has made the classification of research essential. Different authors have classified research in different ways. One hears different types of research such as action research, descriptive research, exploratory research, historical research, comparative research, theory construction, model building, pure research, applied research, operations research, library research, individual research, group research and so on.

The purpose of all research is to discover answers to questions raised by scientists and decision-makers. These people are least bothered about the types of research carried on. The problem of the researcher determines the nature of the enquiry. A brief summary of different types of research is given in the following sections.

2.1 ACTION RESEARCH

The process by which practitioners attempt to study their problems scientifically in order to guide, correct and evaluate their decisions and actions is called action research.

The action research requires the person who faces the problem to find out a solution for it. The following example will clearly explain how action research is conducted. A teacher finds out that most of his pupils are weak in comprehension. This poses a problem to him. He finds out the probable causes for it and guesses that the poor comprehension may be due to the lack of emphasis on developing the following abilities.

(i) Ability to understand vocabulary;

(ii) Ability to follow the organisation of a passage;

(*iii*) Ability to select the main ideas; and

(*iv*) Ability to draw inferences from the passage.

The teacher innovates a method to develop each ability of the student. He develops teaching techniques, observes the response of the pupils and records the data. The records prompt him to conclude that a particular approach is more effective for developing comprehension.

A bus operator wants to study the profitability of the bus operation in the urban and rural areas. For this purpose he selects a town route and mofussil route and ascertains the cost of operation for a month and the collection from the buses. He can compare the routes to find out the more profitable one. His findings will reveal that a particular route is more profitable than the other. This is an action research in the field of business.

2.2 DESCRIPTIVE RESEARCH

A descriptive study may be simple or complex. It determines who, what, when, where and how of a topic. It is concerned with describing the characteristics (e.g., the extent to which libraries are used) estimating the proportion of the people in a specified population who hold certain views or attitudes (e.g., how many favour the abolition of capital punishment?) predicting specifically (e.g., how many will cash their government bonds during a given period?) and discovering or testing whether certain variables are associated (e.g., people who spend a good deal of time for reading, go to movies often with each other).

Descriptive study may employ any of or all the methods of data collection such as interview, questionnaire, observation, tests and cumulative record cards. In the descriptive study the researcher must be careful to make a note of the bias and extravagance that may creep in at every stage of the study—formulating the objectives of the study; designing the methods of data collection; selecting the sample; collecting, processing and analysing the data; and reporting the findings. (For detailed discussion on every stage of research refer to the respective chapters).

In a descriptive study an accurate description of a situation or an association between variables will be emphasized.

2.3 EXPLORATORY STUDIES

When the purpose of research is to gain familiarity with a phenomenon or acquire new insights into it in order to formulate a more precise problem or develop hypothesis, the exploratory studies come in handy. If the theory happens to be too general or too specific, a hypothesis cannot be formulated. Therefore a need for an exploratory research is felt to gain experience that will be helpful in formulating relevant hypothesis for more definite investigation.

For instance, a researcher in the field of Psychology is interested in studying the influence of social environment on mental health. The researcher is restrained from formulating any precise hypothesis for investigation based on the writings on this topic. In such a case the exploratory study is usually most suitable.

The following are the three approaches to the exploratory study.

(1) The Survey of Literature – A review of the literature helps to identify the hypothesis which may serve as a guide for further investigation.

(2) The Experience Survey – A small portion of existing knowledge and experience is put into written form. Everyday experience provides opportunity to obtain information required to formulate hypothesis.

(3) Case Study – The focus may be on individuals or situations or groups or communities. The method of study may lay stress on the examination of the existing records. It may be unstructured interviewing or participant observation or some other approach.

It is important to bear in mind that exploratory study merely leads to insights for formulating hypothesis. Its approaches do not consider it important to test or demonstrate them.

2.4 HISTORICAL RESEARCH

Historical Research is nothing but objective location, evaluation and synthesis of evidence in order to establish facts and draw conclusions concerning the past. Historical method has greater significance for social science research. Many social problems can be adequately analysed only with historical background. In disciplines like Economics, Sociology, Co-operation, Education and Psychology, many studies have employed historical method. To shed light on the cooperative movement in India the researcher has necessarily to resort to the collection of historical data.

The importance of historical research in both basic and applied research in business cannot be understressed. Explanations for the present are derived from historical enquiries. Historical research is concerned with digging up of facts. For example, a study of factors influencing the growth of location for cement plants in Tamil Nadu is an historical research. The factors to be identified by the researcher would be technical, financial, marketing, personnel, political and social. All these factors are of historical value. The evaluation of such research is done by taking into account the source document and the interpretation of the hypothesis.

The main sources of historical data are books, documents, newspapers, magazines, diaries, memoirs, confessions, autobiographies, sacred archieves, suppressed inventions, personal letters, personal agreements, witness, information from person who has made an observation, diplomatic agreements, statistical materials, historical paintings, portraits, charts, maps, inscriptions, monuments, time capsules, carvings and the like.

2.5 COMPARATIVE RESEARCH

This research aims at comparing institutions, practices, concepts, trends in economic variables, economics of different countries and the like over a period of time. For example, a study of the financial performance of two cotton textile mills in terms of profitability over a period of time is comparative study.

Before undertaking the comparative research the following precautions may be taken note of by the researcher.

(i) Collect only necessary data which are useful for comparison.

(ii) Collect only the existing factors and the non-existing factors are to be ignored.

(iii) Draw correct conclusions free from bias.

In undertaking a comparative study the researcher will encounter certain difficulties. Firstly, the researcher cannot formulate a hypothesis to have a specific direction. Secondly, the comparable units are seldom similar. The external factors have greater impact on the units of study which make it to draw a conclusion. Finally, the conclusions drawn in much smaller studies cannot be applied to a wider society or group.

The comparative study may be made very effective if the researcher is fully acquainted with the subjects of his study and makes a good use of his keen power of observation, makes critical appraisal and offers logical explanation.

2.6 THEORY CONSTRUCTION RESEARCH

Theories galore in subjects like Economics, Sociology and Psychology. There are different schools of thought and the views of scholars diverge. A critical evaluation of these views in terms of empirical justification and internal validity is a useful piece of research.

For example, two researchers have been involved in evolving a model for fair rate of return in two engineering units. The two models are very specific in their application. A researcher can compare the models and advantages of the models and state which model is better.

The theories employed to explain the relationship between capital structure, cost of capital and value of the firm are :

(i) Net income approach;

(ii) Net operating income approach;

(iii) Modigliani-Miller (MM) approach; and

(iv) Traditional approach.

Those theories have some assumptions and the theories are discussed in detail in the light of such assumptions. A significant conclusion could be drawn by applying these theories to a practical situation. After comparing the results, the best theory which will be useful in assessing the capital structure, cost of capital and value of the firm will be suggested to be applied to a specific situation.

2.7 MODEL BUILDING RESEARCH

This type of research is mostly done in the field of management. The basic management science represents many theories, which are more complex. The model constructed will show the inter-relationship among many variables and describe the result of research. In the area of business sales forecasting models, advertising models, inventory control models, production control models and capital investment models can be constructed.

2.8 PURE RESEARCH

Pure research is being undertaken to satisfy the researcher's thirst for knowledge and it is mainly goaded by the researcher's curiosity. It may be undertaken for designing tools to tackle practical problems. It is concerned with singular situation and not suitable to a wide area.

J.M. Keynes in his book, *The General Theory of Employment Interest and Money*, published in 1936, explained the ways and means to attain the goal of full employment through the operation of the Central Bank. He has established that by a steady increase in the total spending, the economy can attain the goal of full employment. His theory is applicable to developed economies and not relevant to the developing economies. The findings of the economist have enabled the Americans to revive the economy from the Great Depression of 1930s.

Pure research is largely limited to the academic world. The funds from educational and government institutions and foundations enable researchers to pursue pure research.

Pure research provides the basis for applied research. The principles and laws set up by pure research are applied to the problems arising in the fields of Sociology, Psychology and Economics. Thus pure research enables us to make tools and applied research uses such tools to study a particular case.

2.9 APPLIED RESEARCH

Applied research is undertaken with the aim of uncovering data to solve an existing problem. The driving force of this research is finding solution to a problem. Applied research aims at application of science to a singular situation.

The applied research may be conducted with a view to test the basic assumptions of a theory or validity of a theory. For example, in the field of Economics, a researcher may be interested in applying the Lewis Model to an economy. The researcher may find out why the model has not been applied and what modifications would be required. If the model has been implemented, the researcher will find out how far the model has been implemented. For verifying the applicability of the model a field investigation may be undertaken.

2.10 OPERATIONS RESEARCH

This method of research has been done for solving problems by using scientific methods and quantitative techniques. While the researchers care to study the development of methods, the industrial operations researcher evinces interest in the applications of methods to solve the pressing or critical problems of their firm.

Research can also be classified as conclusion-oriented and decision-oriented. While doing conclusion-oriented research a researcher is free to pick up a problem, redesign the enquiry and is free to conceptualise as he wishes. Decision-oriented research always implies taking a rational decision. Operational research is an example of decision-oriented research.

2.11 LIBRARY RESEARCH

Research investigations may be classified under four general categories namely library research, life and physical science research, social research and technological research.

Library research is conducted with the help of written materials mostly located in large libraries. This research is concerned with the evolution of theories, study involving cause and effect relationship and seeking out significant facts and interpretation of the past data which are found in journals, reports and directories.

2.12 INDIVIDUAL AND GROUP RESEARCH

The research undertaken by an individual is called individual research. The bulk of research activities in universities, and colleges is made by the individual. The individual research is done on the basis of one's own judgement, interest and capacity.

Group research is undertaken by several researchers. Their activities are co-ordinated by a director. Research conducted by a firm, trade association and government agency is performed by a team of researchers under a project director. Research in colleges and universities financed by grants is done on a group basis.

Methods of research may be classified from many points of view such as the fields to which applied, purpose, place where it is conducted, application, data, forms of thinking and control of factors.

3. BUSINESS RESEARCH — ITS NATURE AND SCOPE

Business research is concerned with the operation of business firms and the behaviour of people who comprise them. Business research includes broad topics as behaviour of people in business organisations, business systems analysis, consumer behaviour, economics of business firms and social, political and environmental influences on business firms.

Business research in applied research assumes importance since it is problem-oriented and decision-oriented. Business research normally comes about because a problem exists and therefore there is a need for seeking information by which the problem can be solved. The dynamic nature of the environment in which the research takes place is another feature of business research.

Business research has a wide scope and draws upon the research findings of related disciplines such as Sociology, Psychology, Anthropology, Political Science, Biology, Mathematical and other sciences. Business research may focus on theory or specific operational problems. In the former case the objective would be to discover / illustrate precepts or principles and in the latter case the objective would be to provide solutions to current problems. Topics of research in functional areas of business are given below.

3.1 MARKETING RESEARCH

There is a great need for wide variety of basic research projects in Marketing. The Bible for any research in marketing is the book titled, *The Meaning and Sources of Marketing* by Michael Halbert (McGraw Hill, 1965). There are lots of research topics identified in the field of marketing research. An outline of such topics is given below.

Outline of Marketing Research Topics :

(A) *Marketing Policy*

- *(i)* Pricing
- *(ii)* Advertising
- *(iii)* Service
- *(iv)* Channels of Distribution
- *(v)* Customer Relations

(B) *Product Research*

- *(i)* New Product Ideas
- *(ii)* Market Standardisation and Variety Control
- *(iii)* Improvements and New Uses for Present Products
- *(iv)* Brand Names and Trade Marks
- *(v)* Packaging
- *(vi)* Company and Product Image
- *(vii)* Customer Preferences

(C) *Market Research*

- *(i)* Economic Forecasts
- *(ii)* Industry Forecasts
- *(iii)* Sales Forecasts
- *(iv)* Technology Forecasts
- *(v)* Market and Sales Potential by Product, Customer, Area, Salesmen and Competition

(D) *Sales Management and Methods*

- *(i)* Types of Organisation
- *(ii)* Effectiveness and Efficiency of Sales Organisation
- *(iii)* Customer Service
- *(iv)* Long-range Organisational planning

(E) *Channels of Distribution*

- *(i)* Evaluation of Alternative Channels of Distribution
- *(ii)* Inventory Control

(F) *Advertising and Sales Promotion Research*

- *(i)* Consumer Motivation Studies
- *(ii)* Media Selection
- *(iii)* Advertising Appeals

(iv) Copy Testing
(v) Trade-Show Participation
(vi) Point of Purchase Advertising
(vii) Premiums, Deals and Special Promotions

(Source: Business Research: Concept and Practice Robert G. Murdick, International Text Book Company, 1969, p.23).

3.2 ORGANISATION RESEARCH

Organisation research is a meeting ground for the sociologist, the economist, the political scientist, the operations researcher, the mathematician, the social psychologist and the engineer. Illustrious men of these fields have made a rich contribution to the knowledge about nature and dynamics of organisation.

The organisation research is an inter-disciplinary field. Since the men who do research in organisations, come from a variety of backgrounds they tend to bring with them different tools, different concepts and different methodological approaches.

There is a growing recognition that knowledge of research methods may be useful for students preparing for careers as practising managers. In recent years empirically based knowledge about organisation has grown at a phenomenal rate. The organisation research enables the managers to get exposed to a number of theories and research findings having relevance to organisations.

In many cases the techniques or practices that managers may want to apply in their organisations might have been studied by researchers. For example a manager, who wants to implement staff enrichment, before going in for implementation throughout the organisation, may benefit by the knowledge of research methods.

Although the roles of managers and the research scientists are often viewed as very different, many of the day-to-day problems of managers are similarly to those faced by researchers. If the managers are conversant with the research methods, they can improve their problem-solving efficiency. For example, a manger is confronted with the problem of high absenteeism in one department. Once the problem is identified and the need to take corrective action has been recognised, the manger must collect reliable and authentic information about the problem. The manager may often have hunches about the problem which are similar to the hypothesis of the researcher. If the manager has sound knowledge of research methods, he can scientifically approach the problem. Otherwise, he may try as a fledgling to act on the hunches resulting in an inefficient and costly process of trial and error used while studying a problem. Need hardly be said that a knowledge of research process is highly indispensable to managers.

Research in organisations may be directed towards:

(i) Types of organisations and their effectiveness;

(ii) Behaviour of Employees;

(iii) Development of principles to guide mangers;

(iv) Organisational situation.

Although an accepted theory of management is lacking at this time, the recent research has contributed to our understanding of business organisations. This is a fertile field of research at present.

3.3 INDUSTRIAL RESEARCH

An industrial research laboratory is presumably a pragmatic organisation. Its objectives are directly connected with the future welfare of a particular company. The specific objectives of industrial research are the following :

(i) To improve the quality of products;

(ii) To develop new materials, processes or devices for capturing new markets;

(iii) To develop new uses for existing materials, processes or devices;

(iv) To effect savings in cost;

(v) To abate dangers;

(vi) To assist in standardisation; and

(vii) To improve customer and public relations.

3.4 PRODUCTION RESEARCH

A good production organisation is never static. It keeps on changing. If the production unit is successful, the changes turn about to be improvements. But the changes always bring difficulties, if not troubles. Thus the research laboratory plays a logical and continuing role of production research in the production picture.

Production research activities normally fall into three classifications :

(i) Investigation of new production methods

(ii) Investigation of methods of standardisation and control

(iii) Specialised "trouble shooting".

4. BENEFITS OF RESEARCH

Research is essentially an investigation, a recording and an analysis of evidence for the purpose of gaining knowledge. In other words, research is an organised enquiry to find out facts. The inherent aim of every research is gaining knowledge. Knowledge is a tool to solve the problems of individuals, institutions, and the society at large.

In research problem means a question which is put forward to be answered. In business there are plenty of problems which require immediate solution. The problems may be pertaining to production, marketing, finance and the like. These problems need immediate solution and the research and development wing of the business organisation offer the enterprise expertise to solve such problems.

Man is a social animal. He is always sagacious and has developed an enquiring mind. He is prompted to ask so many questions such as what, why and how of a thing. His unquenchable eagerness spurs him to find answers to such questions. The renowned scientist, Isaac Newton chanced to observe the apples falling down from the apple tree and developed many enquiries. These enquiries enabled Isaac Newton to propound the law of gravitation. Thus research questions give birth to new ideas, new products, new theories, and new concepts.

A burning thirst for knowledge fires many people with new knowledge and could quench their thirst. Research enlightens such people and satisfies their thirst for knowledge.

The benefits of research to the society are numerous. Some of the benefits of research are listed below :

4.1 ADDITION TO EXISTING LITERATURE

Many books have come out of research conducted in various fields. A book is not a talked thing, but a written thing; and written, not with the view of mere communication but with the aim of offering new insights into unknown spheres of human life. Books of this kind have been written in all ages by great leaders, great statesmen and great thinkers. The researchers add lot of new books to the library; new concepts have been developed and the implication of such concepts in various literature has been studied in depth. The outcome of such studies is the production of plenty of books.

Prof. Galbraith, former American ambassador in India started writing his book, *The New Industrial State* in 1957 but it was published in 1967. He found out that spontaneity comes into his writing only in the fourth and fifth draft. He therefore kept on working on the theme. A preliminary draft was prepared in 1961. But then suddenly he was summoned to take up ambassadorship in India. He put away the precious manuscripts in a vault of a bank. After the tenure of ambassador, he developed it and published it and the book proved to be the world best-seller. Plenty of books have been written on the basis of investigation.

4.2 SCIENTIFIC INVENTION

Research may be pure or applied. Pure research is done in colleges and universities in large scale and the findings of such studies will be the basis for applied research. In the field of medicine and engineering a lot of inventions have been made and such inventions ensured to people sound health and longevity.

A group of engineering students of Bangalore has come out with a technical change in the bicycle recently. They have modified a conventional bicycle into what they call a "Jogging or oscillating pedal" type by replacing the rotating pedal with a jogging pedal. The students claim that this conversion has the mechanical advantage of making cycling less strenuous.

The scientific invention that a child can be grown in a test tube popularly known as 'Test Tube Baby', has enabled many couples to have children.

4.3 INTELLECTUAL SATISFACTION

Unquestionably research enables a person to attain intellectual satisfaction. Dr. Chandrasekar who has been awarded Nobel Prize for his thesis, "How stars are born and what they are made of" stated that he worked for personal satisfaction. As usual his work could command public appreciation only after some length of time.

Father Artwell did a novel research in Bible for his personal satisfaction. He found out that Bible consists of 35,66,480 letters and 7,73,693 words. The word "Lord" has been used 1,855 times and the word "And" 46,277 times. This type of research gives mental satisfaction to the researcher.

4.4 RESEARCH IS A TOOL OF SOCIAL TRANSFORMATION

In social research the problems of the society are given top most priority and the current social problems are taken up for an indepth study. In the process of identification, selection and formulation of the research problems, the researcher has social interaction with people of different backgrounds.

At the stage of collection of data with the help of an interview schedule, a questionnaire and a check-list, the researcher has the chance of educating the respondent. The outlook of the respondent changes tremendously while furnishing information. For example a researcher interested in studying the problem of bonded labour, not only collects data regarding bonded labour but also impresses upon the bonded labourers the need for freeing themselves from the bondage of the landlords.

4.5 RESEARCH SHARPENS THE MIND

Observation is the basic method of obtaining information around us. It is seeing things with a purpose. It is in fact looking closely and purposefully. There are three components in observation, namely sensation, attention and perception. Sensation is the first step. Observations are gained through organs. The reliability and fullness of sensory reactions depend upon sensory organs. Hence the investigator should be physically sound. The second ingredient is the investigator's ability to pursue the subject under study. Concentration in the initial stages is a matter of will power. But in due course the training, experience, and grit could make it almost a matter of habit. The third element perception comprises the interpretation of the sensory reports. The observation trains the sensory organs and disciplines the mind to concentrate. This exercise sharpens the mind and endows it with enormous powers to take a rational decision.

Besides the benefits listed above, research brings reputation to the institution to which the researcher belongs. It gives a promising career and recognition to researchers. Better business decisions can be taken with the help of operations research. Feasibility studies such as technical feasibility, economic feasibility, financial feasibility and commercial feasibility of projects can be undertaken effectively by the researchers.

REFERENCES

1. Marie Jahoda, Morton Deutsch and Stuart W. Cook, *Research Methods in Social Relations* (New York : Holt, Rineholt and Winston, 1959), p.2.
2. Fred Kerlinger, *Foundation of Behavioural Research* (New York: Holt, Rineholt and Wineholt and Winston, 1964), p. 456.
3. William Emory, C., *Business Research Methods* (Ontario: Irwin-Dorsey Limited, 1976), p.8.
4. Rummel, J.F., and Rallaine W.C., *Research Methodology in Business* (New York : Harper & Row, 1963), p.2.
5. Robert Ross, *Research — An Introduction* (New York : Banes and Noble Books, 1974), p.3.
6. Gopal M.H., *An Introduction to Research Procedure in Social Sciences* (Madras : Asia Publishing House, 1970), p.4.
7. Richard T. Mowday and Richard M. Steers, *Research in Organisations* (California: Goodyear Publishing Company, Inc., 1970), p.2.
8. Rummel, J.F., and Ballaine, W.C. *op.cit.*, p.4.

CHAPTER TWO

PLANNING RESEARCH PROJECT

1. *Identification of Research Problems*
2. *Selection of a Problem*
3. *Formulation of a Problem*
4. *Research Design*
5. *A Model Design*

1. IDENTIFICATION OF RESEARCH PROBLEMS

Research may be motivated by the desire to know for the sake of knowing or by the desire to solve practical problems. The researcher, who is associated with practical problems, need not identify problems, since he has many problems on hand. But the researcher, who is associated with academic institutions, has to identify possible problems for investigation.

In simple words problem means a question thrown forward for solution. A problem exists when an individual interacts with his environment and finds himself in an indeterminate situation, or in a state of questioning, doubting or uncertainty.

Problems may be classified as conceptual problems, which can be solved by creative thinking, selection and synthesis, logical problems, which are solved by deductive methods and empirical problems, which are solved by inductive reasoning based upon observation of phenomena.

In specific problem-solving research, a research is concerned with application of research methods to find satisfactory solution to a pressing problem. In a business there are numerous problems which need solutions. As the resources are limited, it is indispensable to identify only the important problems. In the field of academic research also, the researcher will be able to identify several problems but he can screen them out by preliminary selection.

A problem clearly and accurately stated is a problem that is often well on its way to being solved. Before research or fact finding can successfully start, the investigator must know what the problem is and why a solution is wanted. The 'what' of a problem is answered by an accurate definition of the situation. The 'why' can be established by the determination of the uses to which the findings will be or can be put.

The following approaches may be used to find problem areas. Now let us study in detail the different approaches.

1.1 ASK EXPERTS

If the problems are to be identified, ask experts in the area of research. The researcher can attend professional society meetings and listen to the business executives. The researcher can also interview the executives and thus he can be conversant with various issues.

1.2 BECOME A SPECIALIST

Knowledge knows no bounds. It is very difficult to acquire knowledge in a wide area of study. Therefore the researcher may select a narrow area of both theoretical and practical significance. He can make himself an expert in the field through course work and independent reading.

1.3 SEARCH THE LITERATURE

The researcher should read professional journals in his area of concentration, masters' theses, doctoral dissertations, research reports and government publications. Through the survey of literature the researcher will discover unanswered questions which require answer, the solutions of various scholars to the same problem and research studies in progress at other institutions on the same problems.

1.4 EXPLORE AREAS OF DISSATISFACTION

The researcher should read critical articles appearing in periodicals and newspapers. He should discuss the issues with professors and colleagues and listen to their critical points of view. The critical articles and discussions will enable the researcher to identify many possible problems.

1.5 LOOK FOR CURRENT DEVELOPMENTS

The current developments in a particular field of specialisation provide scope for many topics. For instance, installation of electronic computer in business establishments suggests a number of topics for research. The bank rate increase of the Reserve Bank of India has created impact on the different economic activities of the country, giving scope for many topics for research.

1.6 MAINTAIN A DIARY

The researcher should keep a diary and jot down questions and ideas that strike him. In the course of his reading, discussion with his colleagues, in having contacts with business executives and in meditative moment, the curious and scientifically oriented researcher will always be wondering and critically evaluating. He has to document the ideas. If any idea flashes in his mind, he should jot it down on any piece of paper available.

1.7 EXAMINE THE GAP BETWEEN THEORY AND PRACTICE

The researcher may identify problems by re-examining the theoretical structure of the area of research in which he is interested. He may also find the gap between theory and practice. Afterwards, the researcher may find out the way to bridge the gap between theory and practice.

In many parts of the world, a student undertakes Ph.D. programme only after writing scores of term papers and a dozen of seminar papers. There are many periodicals in our country today which are eager to get articles and publish at regular intervals, say weekly, fortnightly, monthly and the like. There are plenty of opportunities available to the students to write articles in college magazines and souvenirs. If the students follow such practice they will not find it difficult to identify possible research problems for a study.

1.8 LOCATING THE PROBLEM IN A FIRM

All the managerial techniques of control and direction that are appropriate for the operation of a firm under consideration would provide information in search for possible problems that might call for research. The following devices and techniques can become the effective ways of finding problems.

1. Study the records and reports of the firms.
2. Careful observation of conditions in the firm.
3. Purposeful conversation with other qualified persons in the firm.

4. Careful observation and study of the procedures and techniques of the best, efficient and successful firms in the industry.
5. Reading of pertinent published materials.
6. Use of checklists in evaluating the operations of a firm.
7. Brain storming – intensified discussion with the group of interested persons.

A checklist consisting of a detailed listing of all the pertinent areas of the operations of a business firm shall be constructed. The process of constructing a checklist stimulates thinking and results in more clear and logical consideration of the problem. The checklist should be simple and short.

2. SELECTION OF A PROBLEM

A research problem rightly and rationally selected helps the researcher to complete the project within the prescribed time limit and the budgeted amount. The right selection of a research problem will boost the morale of the researcher. In the selection of a problem a researcher should take in consideration the following factors.

2.1 RESEARCHER'S INTEREST

The researcher should possess probing attitude, tenacity of spirit and dedication to thoroughness. A researcher will be able to imbibe these three virtues, if he has personal interest in the results of study. If the researcher has little interest, the project will become a sheer drudgery.

2.2 TOPIC OF SIGNIFICANCE

If a student selects a problem which could be applied in practice, he may be able to attract the attention of the people in the practical field of study. The results of the study will also be used by the people in the business. If the student selects a significant theoretical problem, he can keep in touch with leading scholars in the field. The constant touch of the researcher with scholars will stimulate his thinking and enthusiasm.

2.3 NOVELTY OF THE IDEA

A novel problem may offer scope for new ways of looking at the problem. A novel problem conceived by the researcher is a sign ensuring his promising research career.

2.4 RESEARCHER'S RESOURCES

The resources of the researcher are his intelligence, training and experience and other facilities such as funds, clerical and technical assistance, library facilities and availability of time. Time is the foremost factor in choosing a problem. A research can be conducted within three months and the same research can be pursued for three years also. Therefore, the topic must be selected in such a way as to enable the researcher to finish the study within the prescribed period.

In a social research, library resources such as books, journals, periodicals, research reports, research journals, professional journals, bibliographies and indices constitute the flesh and blood of research. If library resources are poor, the researcher has to select a problem for which he can gather primary data.

2.5 AVAILABILITY OF DATA

The researcher has to examine whether the data for the project are available in plenty. If the study is based on secondary data, the researcher has to find out whether the data is within his reach. If the research is based on primary data, the researcher has to see whether the respondents will answer the questions. It will be difficult to obtain sensitive data such as sales, profit and union-management relations.

2.6 BENEFITS OF THE RESEARCH

The results of a research study may give intellectual satisfaction to the researcher. He gets recognition for his work from his colleagues and outside scholars. The researcher can also publish his thesis. The institutions sponsoring research studies derive benefit from the study. The research study is a service done to the profession, institution and society. All these provide a strong motivation to select a problem and pursue research.

2.7 FEASIBILITY OF THE STUDY

The factors such as availability of equipments, subjects, library facilities and time should be noted before selecting a problem.

A researcher need not be in a hurry in choosing a problem. Spending considerable time in selecting a topic would not be a waste at all. It could save enormous time in the later stages.

A young researcher is often tempted to think that his study must result in some extra-ordinary findings. Too high ambition in this sphere is dangerous, since it may lead to the selection of an unmanageable problem. Today a thesis is judged not in terms of its revolutionary findings and original discoveries, but in terms of the candidate's methods of work and analytical abilities.

Social scientists with different values choose different topics for investigation. They should guard against bias which might enter into their research. Personal whims of the researchers inevitably influence the choice of the topic. The only means by which the rationality of scientific procedure can be maintained is the awareness as to where and how the bias creeps in.

3. FORMULATION OF A PROBLEM

Formulation of a research problem is translating and transforming the selected problem into a scientific research question. A problem well put is half solved. There are seven factors strengthening such careful formulation.

(i) Proper formulation of the problem provides a sense of direction to the research;

(ii) Proper formulation specifies the scope of research;

(iii) Proper formulation indicates the limitations of the research;

(iv) Proper formulation clarifies the problem;

(v) Proper formulation establishes the major assumptions;

(vi) Proper formulation expresses the context of the problem;and

(vii) Proper formulation provides economy in research.

Having identified a problem area, the researcher proceeds to develop and define the problem statement. He has to follow the following three methods in formulating the problem.

(i) Narrowing down from general and vague to more specific statements.

(ii) Oscillating between over broad and over narrow.

(iii) Broadening a narrow specific question into a broader significant problem.

3.1 STEPS IN FORMULATION

A researcher has to follow the undermentioned steps one by one in formulating a research problem.

3.1.1 DEVELOPING A TITLE

The title of the study indicates the intention of the researcher and shows the focus of the study. It reveals whether the study is a case, a statistical, exploratory, formalised and observational survey, descriptive, casual and experimental study or simulation. The title should be specific.

3.1.2 WORKING OUT CONCEPTUAL MODEL

A problem may be selected from theory or ideas derived from theory. Once a problem area is conceived, the researcher could develop and define the problem statement. He has to narrow down from general and vague to more specific statements. Sometimes he has to broaden a narrow specific question into a broader significant problem.

3.1.3 DEFINING THE OBJECTIVES

The researcher must first of all decide the questions to be answered. Then he has to decide whether the study is descriptive or analytical. the researcher has to find answers to the following questions.

(i) What data are available or obtainable?

(ii) What are the constraints?

(iii) Can any constraints be modified or removed?

3.1.4 LIMITING THE SCOPE

The researcher must demarcate the geographical limits, time limit and magnitude of the problem.

3.1.5 FORMULATION OF HYPOTHESIS

Hypothesis is a proposition or principle which is assumed in order to draw logical conclusions. Hypothesis is a provisional idea based on limited amount of evidence. Once a hypothesis is tested with the help of evidence, it becomes a thesis. Hypothesis gives direction to research.

3.1.6 OPERATIONAL DEFINITION OF CONCEPTS

The operational definition enables to form specific ideas regarding the data needed. A word gives multiple meanings. For example, a student of sociology must know that culture refers to the totality of the social heritage of any society. On the other hand, the word, "culture" has different meaning in Bacteriology. So the researcher must be very careful in giving the operational definition.

3.2 FORMULATION OF PROBLEM — A CASE

A problem formulation is a ticklish problem in research. The following case will enlighten the researcher regarding the formulation of a problem by narrowing down from a broad area.

Mr. X wanted to pursue research leading to Ph.D. degree. He had no idea as to what field or topic he was going to write on. He had some interest in accounting area and therefore he had decided to write a thesis in the area of accounting. He had decided to read some articles in the field but not yet decided his research topic. In the area of Accounting, he did some more reading. As a result, he was able to identify some fields of study.

(i) Pension plans;

(ii) Extra-Ordinary gains and losses; and

(iii) Accounting ethics.

Out of these three topics, the researcher selected pension plans. He had been reading articles in this area but had not narrowed this topic down to anything specific. Tentatively he planned to find out the trend pertaining to the financing and accounting of pension plans. The researcher wanted to find out how companies are financing and accounting their pension plans. He had read most of the articles in the library relating to financing and accounting of pension. He wrote the project proposal with the help of his colleagues and after a good deal of discussion he had narrowed down his topic to the financing of pension plans. He prepared the research design on the topic "The Financing of Pension Plans."

A researcher is a very important person. The responsibilities he has to shoulder are to identify problems, select a problem and formulate the selected problem. The shouldering of responsibility mainly depends upon the interest of the researcher. The interest in research is developed out of certain inherent qualities of man. Reward is not always the only incentive to work. At the University of Pisa, Galileo developed interest in Mathematics and gave up pre-medical studies. He was not interested in monetary rewards. In those days a Professor of Medicine received Rs. 9,000 a year and a Professor of Mathematics only about Rs. 300.

The great scientist Dr. Chandrasekar, who has written his thesis on "How stars are born and what these are made of," opined that he worked for his personal satisfaction on things generally outside the scientific mainstream.

It is impossible to set forth any rigid formulation of methods or procedures to be followed by all researchers. The researchers, the research undertakings and the conditions and circumstances are not alike. Therefore, it is not possible to follow a formula or standard procedure in all circumstances.

4. RESEARCH DESIGN

After selecting the topic, the researcher has to plan how he should conduct his research in the most efficient and successful manner. Good planning gives the researcher direction for the successful completion of the project. The plan of study is called research design.

Research Design is the blue print of the proposed study. It represents the overall scheme of the study. "A research design is a logical and systematic planning and it helps directing a piece of research."

In planning the research project the researcher should identify the data to be used, and state how they are to be collected, how they can be classified and how they are analysed. The working out of a plan involves making decisions with respect to the following questions.

(i) What is the study about?

(ii) Why is the study being made?

(iii) What types of data are needed?

(iv) Where can the needed data be found?

(v) What are the sources of data?

(vi) What periods of time will the study include?

(vii) How many cases will be covered?

(viii) What basis of selection will be used?

(ix) What techniques of gathering data will be followed?

(x) How will the data be processed?

(xi) What methods of analysis will be adopted?

(xii) To what type of audience is its reporting meant?

(xiii) What kind of report will be prepared?

The decisions in respect of the above questions constitute the body of the research design.

The researcher has to take great care in the preparation of the research design. In the beginning this plan is generally vague and tentative and it undergoes many modifications and changes as the study progresses.

4.1 COMPONENTS OF RESEARCH DESIGN

The research design should contain the following elements.

4.1.1 TITLE OF THE STUDY

Enough information should be given in the title, to identify the study. The researcher should consider the following while selecting a title.

(i) The title should be specific to the area of the study.

(ii) The title should indicate the topic of the study.

(iii) The language of the title should be professional in nature but not pedantic.

(iv) The title should be as brief as possible.

4.1.2 INTRODUCTION

Under this heading a brief explanation of the genesis of the problem should be given.

4.1.3 STATEMENT OF THE PROBLEM

After a brief introduction explaining the genesis of the problem, the researcher should state the problem. While stating the problem use of clear, simple and concise statement is preferable.

4.1.4 REVIEW OF PREVIOUS STUDIES

Under this head the researcher presents what is so far known about the problem under consideration. All related studies need not be discussed. the researcher may describe the most important ones. A review of the previous studies enables the researcher to know the different areas covered by various studies, to concentrate on the areas where little research has been carried out, to look into various merits and shortcomings of certain studies already completed and to verify the present findings with that of the previous ones.

4.1.5 SCOPE OF THE STUDY

This heading gives an idea about the extent of the study. The scope of the study is dependent on several factors such as the time and money available with the investigator, availability of the sample, co-operation of the respondents and the like.

4.1.6 OBJECTIVES OF THE STUDY

The task of the researcher is to lay down the objectives precisely. The objectives enlighten the researcher's own mind and lead to more efficient enquiry. Once the objectives are settled, the study can be undertaken with required accuracy and within the given resources. The objectives mentioned should be well within the scope of the study.

4.1.7 HYPOTHESIS TO BE TESTED

Hypothesis is a proposition, condition or principle which is assumed, perhaps without belief in order to draw logical conclusions. Hypotheses are formulated to explain observed facts, conditions, or behaviours and to serve as a guide in the research process. Each hypothesis is individually tested to determine whether it is tenable or not. Hypothesis should be stated in clear, concise and understandable language.

4.1.8 OPERATIONAL DEFINITION OF CONCEPTS

All terms that might be ambiguous should be clarified. A clear understanding of the terms used in the study is important. It is necessary to identify and label the variables. The variables can be labelled as independent variable and dependent variable. An independent variable is that factor which is measured, manipulated or selected by the experiments. A dependent variable is that factor which is measured to determine the effect of independent variable.

4.1.9 GEOGRAPHICAL AREA TO BE COVERED

Under this head the area to be covered by the study is mentioned.

4.1.10 REFERENCE PERIOD

The period of the study can be mentioned under this heading.

4.1.11 METHODOLOGY

The researcher should first determine the kind of information needed to answer the research questions. Secondly he must know the sources of data and finally he must know the means by which he will gather information which is known as methodology.

4.1.12 SAMPLING

Sampling involves taking a portion of population, making observation on this smaller group and then generalising the findings to be applied to a large population. The small group that is observed is called the sample and the large group is called population. the sample is the portion of the population and it must be representative of the population. If the sample is biased, the findings of the study cannot be generalised.

4.1.13 TOOLS FOR COLLECTION OF DATA

The choice of method for collecting the data is governed by the subject matter, the unit of enquiry and the scale of study. A study of the behaviour of a group would call for observational techniques. for a simple enquiry among the cross section of population, a questionnaire is adequate. A survey of general population entailing many complicated questions would call for personal interviewing.

4.1.14 PLAN OF ANALYSIS

Once the data have been collected, they must be reduced to meaningful results by statistical analysis so that the conclusion for generalisation can be drawn from them. The researcher should describe how he plans to organise the data. He should decide the statistical treatment. The appropriateness of the techniques should be discussed. He must discuss the procedure for treating the data.

4.1.15 RESEARCH REPORT

The results should be communicated. The format consists of three parts.

Part I Preliminary pages, which contain title page, approval sheet, preface (if any), table of contents, list of tables (if any) and list of figures (if any).

Part II Body of the Report, which covers content chapters.

Part III Supplementary pages which include bibliography appendix (if any) and index (if any).

4.1.16 TIME SCHEDULE

The researcher has to work out a time schedule for his research work. The time required includes the following :

(i) Time to be used for preparing the theoretical background;

(ii) Time to be used for preparing the data gathering devices such as questionnaire, interview schedule, record sheet, interviewer's manual and time and expenses sheets;

(iii) Time to be used for data collection;

(iv) Time to be used for processing the data;

(v) Time to be used for writing the report;

(vi) Time to be used for submitting the thesis.

4.1.17 FINANCIAL BUDGET

It is desirable to work out the budget which gives an idea about the money needed to complete the project. The cost estimates of the project will include stationery, printing, sample selection, field work, mailing, processing, tabulating, preparation of report and overheads.

The Research designs will differ depending on the research purpose. The research purposes may purport to gain familiarity with a phenomenon, portray accurately the characteristics of a particular individual, situation or group, determine the frequency with which something occurs and test a hypothesis of casual relationship between variables. In practice, these different types of studies are not always sharply distinguishable. The research design will be more or less the same for any type of study.

5. A MODEL DESIGN[1]

5.1 INTRODUCTION

The origin and growth of the small scale industry in India, as it is known today, may be traced to the industrial policies of the Government of India from time to time since Independence.

The first Industrial Policy Resolution of 6th April 1948 passed by the Government of India has stressed the importance of small scale industries in the development of the national economy of the country. The resolution states that the cottage and small industries were particularly suited for better utilisation of local resources and for the achievement of local self-sufficiency in respect of certain types of essential consumer goods. It has also recognised the need for safeguards against intensive competition by large scale manufacturer. In pursuance of this policy, the Government of India has taken several concrete measures to develop the small scale industry.

The second Industrial Policy Resolution of the Government of India dated 30th April 1956 has made a categorical enunciation of state policies towards the development of the small industries. The policy emphasised the need for self-supporting growth of small scale industry and its integration with large scale industries. This policy was implemented on the eve of launching the Second Five Year Plan (1956-61) which has programmed the development of small scale industries. The Third Five Year Plan (1961-66) aimed at greater diversification of production in the small scale sector and closer integration between the large and small sectors in specified items such as agricultural implements and machines, bicycles and cycle parts, sewing machines, automobile and diesel engine spares, and radio receivers and amplifiers. During the Fourth Five Year Plan (1969-74) 14 major commercial banks were nationalised and this has helped the acceleration of the flow of funds from the banks to the small scale sector.

In 1970, the Government of India announced a new licencing policy which reiterated the policy of reservation of certain items (47 items as per the Industrial Policy Resolution of 1956) and eight more items such as cycle tyres and tubes, tooth-paste, steel furniture, mechanical toys and electrical toys, electrical horns, hydraulic jacks (below 30 tonnes capacity), aluminium utensils and fountain pens have been reserved for small scale industry. The policy envisaged that the list of reserved items would be expanded progressively depending upon the ability of the small scale industries to produce goods economically.

The Industrial Policy of 1977 has laid stress on the effective promotion of small scale industries and their dispersal in rural areas and reservation of 504 items (later reclassified to include 807 items) to small scale industries. With a view to implementing the policy, a new institutional framework titled District Industries Centre was envisaged to create linkages between the government and other allied agencies and small entrepreneurs.

The policy statement made by the Government of India in 1980 has emphasised the need for harmonious growth of small and large scale industries by "fostering complementarity" between the large and small sectors so that the dichotomies between the two sectors do not destroy the economic pattern. The Japanese experience has amply proved that such planned complementarity would help the industrial development of any country and that their co-existence is a reality through mutual dependence. Majority of the small firms in Japan function as ancillaries to large firms and their share in the total industrial output is about 30 per cent.

5.2 STATEMENT OF THE PROBLEM

The growth of small scale industry is vital to the country from three angles. Firstly through the growth of small scale industry regional development could be achieved to a considerable extent. Secondly, this sector would be able to provide employment opportunities to skilled and unskilled manpower not absorbed by large scale sector. Lastly, the sector would help the growth of large scale industry by providing necessary support through ancillary activities.

The above role of the small scale industry is reflected in the three groups of small industries in existence in India which are :

(i) Those in which small scale production has certain advantages and is not affected by large scale industry to any great extent;

(ii) Those in which small scale industry is concerned with the manufacture of certain parts or with certain stages of production in a manufacturing process in which the predominant role is that of large scale industry; and

(iii) Those in which small scale industry has to meet the competition of the corresponding large scale industry.

The first group of units is quite independent of large scale units. The growth of those units is in no way affected by the latter. They can be started anywhere.

The third group of units, being competitive in nature, will have to face stiff competition from the large scale units which enjoy the economies of large scale operations. The survival of this group mainly depends upon its ability to meet the challenges of the market or it should enjoy some kind of protection from the competition of large scale units.

It is the second group of small scale units whose growth and survival depend on its relationship with large scale units. For a country like India the overall growth of small scale sector is very important. Firstly, the sector is less capital-intensive. Secondly it needs minimum infrastructure facilities for growth. Thirdly, in its expansion, dispersed industrial development can be achieved. Lastly, it has every potential to generate employment opportunities according to regional needs. Due to these merits the small scale sector, has been enjoying the support of the government in the form of liberalised import licences, marketing assistance, reservation of certain industrial activities to the small scale sector, hire-purchase of machinery through National Small Industries Corporation, setting up of industrial estates, technical assistance through Small Industries Service Institutes, liberal financial assistance through State Finance Corporations and public and private sector banks, special incentives for location in backward areas and setting up of District Industries Centres. Apart from these measures, priority in the supply of raw materials, supply of power at cheaper rates and the like have also contributed to the growth of small scale industries.

Although all the steps taken by the Government of India to promote small scale industry in the country are commendable, some of them are questionable on economic grounds. The survival of small scale units in the absence of large scale economies is doubtful due to inflationary conditions. Secondly, competition of small scale units with large scale units is difficult, if not impossible. Thirdly, competition of small scale units enjoying protection is a myth. Lastly, encouragement of small scale industry at any cost is detrimental to the interest of the community as it has to pay for the diseconomies.

Hence a more pragmatic approach is necessary if small scale industry has to play a useful role in the economy and there should be rethinking as to the tasks to be assigned to the sector.

With the avowed policy of the Government of India for planned industrial development with particular reference to basic industries and engineering Industries, the third group of industries have gained importance as feeder units to large scale units manufacturing capital goods such as machine tools, bicycles, automobiles, railway equipment and electrical and electronic appliances. Obviously, there is a cause of the co-existence of both small industries and large scale industries in the country as independent integral parts. To provide a strong base for such co-existence of small and large scale units, the complementary aspects of both types are to be identified "so that both of them can contribute equally to the total development of the country."

The large scale units can help the speedy growth of small scale units if they purchase their requirements from the small scale units. The experience of Japan bears testimony to the inter-relationship of small scale units with the large ones. A large part of Japan's population is drawn into labour-intensive small scale units, which exist side by side with large scale units. This co-existence of small and large industries is responsible for the industrialisation of Japan. Thus the small enterprises contribute to the economy both directly and indirectly; but mainly through large scale industry. The purchases made by large scale units from the small ones promote inter-relationship between small and large scale units. This relationship will grow stronger and stronger if the small scale units meet the requirements of the large scale units satisfactorily.

The inter-relationship of small scale units with large ones has been observed to be existing largely in the engineering industry in Coimbatore. The small scale engineering units of Coimbatore manufacture accessories and components for textile machinery, pumpsets, diesel engines, motors, agricultural implements and lathes manufactured by large scale units. It has been observed that many factors have contributed to the inter-relationship of small scale units with large ones, thereby ensuring their peaceful co-existence. This raises the following issues:

(i) What is the extent of inter-relationship of small scale units with large ones?

(ii) What are the factors that have contributed to such inter-relationship?

(iii) What are the benefits of such inter-relationship accruing to small scale units?

These are some questions which require investigation. If empirical foundation is made available, it may help to frame future industrial policy of the country. It is by nature both descriptive and analytical.

5.3 REVIEW OF THE PREVIOUS STUDIES

This research is the first of its kind and it attempts to analyse the inter-relationship of small scale units with large ones. There are many studies on the organisation and management of small scale units. Although they do not have any direct bearing on the subject of research, the methodology and findings of those works have been quite useful.

The study undertaken by Jadavpur University under the auspices of the Reserve Bank of India titled "Survey of Small Engineering Units in Howrah" has yielded detailed data on the technical and economic aspects of small engineering units such as capital, labour costs and output, net value added and its distribution among labour and capital (financial) personnel, works management and marketing organisation. An outstanding feature brought to light by the survey is the close interdependence among units and the fact that they are in the practice of placing order with neighbours.

Dr. Sharad Kopardekar D. has made a study on small scale industries in Poona with special reference to investment and output aspects. The study has thrown light on the factors affecting their growth and productivity and suggests measures to improve their growth and productivity. In the study, "Scope for ancillary industries in and around Hyderabad", undertaken by SIET Institute, a systematic survey of medium and large scale industries has been undertaken in and around Hyderabad with a view to guide new entrepreneurs in establishing ancillary industries in and around Hyderabad.

With the combined efforts of both the Tamil Nadu Small Industries Development Corporation and the Small Industries Service Institute,

Madras a study titled "Scope for small scale industries in Tamil Nadu" has been undertaken for the benefit of potential entrepreneurs of the State of Tamil Nadu. This study provides market data in respect of many engineering and non-engineering units which can be profitably set up in Tamil Nadu.

The study titled "Entrepreneurship in Small Scale Industries in Madurai City and its Environs," undertaken by Gandhigram Institute of Rural Higher Education, has highlighted the characteristics of the entrepreneurs of small scale industries in Madurai City and its environs and the factors that have encouraged small entrepreneurship.

The study "Industrial Entrepreneurship in Madras State," undertaken by Dr. Berna, has reveled that medium size manufacturing firms have grown from humble beginnings. Another interesting finding is that the entrepreneurs responsible for the growth of medium scale firms have come from a wide range of social and economic backgrounds.

In his study titled "Indian Basic Industries — A Study in Growth and Inter-industry relationships," Yadava Reddy has studied the growth and the inter-industry relationship of basic industries, heavy engineering industries and basic consumption goods industries. The main finding of the study is that the rate of growth of basic consumption goods industries has not developed in a balanced manner. This gives a clue that to overcome the shortcomings, it would be better to develop meaningful integration of activities by assigning certain areas of production to small scale sector.

The study "An Empirical Study of Small Scale Industries in Poona – A Study in Structural Analysis of Costs," undertaken by Ashok Joshi, has attempted to examine the effect of impact of cost information on decision making and the potentiality of the Break-Even analysis to appraise cost performance of small scale units.

The study undertaken by Ommen MA titled "Small Scale Industries in Kerala — A Case Study of the Role of Industries in Economic Growth" purports to examine the extent to which the various objectives of small scale industry programmes have been realised in Kerala. A detailed study of industrial estates, rural industries projects, special programmes of assistance in the field of finance and marketing and other services has been undertaken.

Prof. K.T. Ramakrishna in his study titled "Finance for Small Scale Industry in India", has described the nature of problems of finance in regard to small scale industry in India and the role played by the Government, State Financial Corporations and Banks in financing the small scale units. The thesis has also highlighted the methods of financing followed by several countries such as Japan, USA, UK, Europe, Canada, Australia, Asia and Latin America.

5.4 SCOPE OF THE STUDY

This study has been made to analyse the factors influencing the interrelationship of small scale units with the large scale ones and the extent of such relationships. It also analyses the benefits accruing to small scale units as a result of such interrelationship.

The approach to the study has been from the point of view of small engineering units and not from the point of view of large engineering units.

The study has been undertaken mainly to measure the trends of interrelationship of small scale units with large scale units but not to form an estimate.

The study pertaining to the benefits of interrelationship has been based mainly on qualitative data as quantitative data are not available since the small scale units do not maintain records systematically.

5.5 OBJECTIVES OF THE STUDY

The study has the following objectives :

(i) To study the progress of small scale industry in Coimbatore District and Tamil Nadu with special reference to engineering industry.

(ii) To measure the degree of interrelationship of small scale engineering units with large scale engineering units.

(iii) To identify the factors influencing the interrelationship of small scale engineering units with large scale engineering units.

(iv) To study the benefits of interrelationship accruing to small scale engineering units.

(v) To offer suggestions for achieving higher degree of interrelationship of small scale engineering units with large scale engineering units.

5.6 HYPOTHESES

The study aims at testing the following hypotheses in line with the objectives mentioned above.

(i) Technical qualifications of small entrepreneurs do not promote interrelationship of small scale units with large scale units.

(ii) Previous employment of small entrepreneurs in large scale units does not promote interrelationship of small scale units with large scale units.

(iii) Nearness to large scale units does not promote interrelationship of small scale units with large scale units.

(iv) Nature of products of small units does not promote interrelationship of small scale units with large scale units.

(v) Period of relationship between small scale units and large scale units does not promote interrelationship of small scale units with large scale units.

(vi) Communal identity of entrepreneurs of small and large scale units does not promote interrelationship of small scale units with large scale units.

(vii) Personal interaction of entrepreneurs of small scale units with large ones through school/college peer groups does not promote interrelationship of small scale units with large scale units.

(viii) Social relationship of small entrepreneurs with the executive of large scale units does not promote interrelationship of small units with large scale units.

(ix) Training facilities made available in large scale units for the employees of small scale units do not promote interrelationship of small scale units with large scale units.

(x) Erstwhile employees of small scale units becoming entrepreneurs in large scale units do not promote interrelationship of small scale units with the large scale units.

(xi) Issue of certificate of order by large scale units to entrepreneurs of small scale units does not promote interrelationship of small scale units with large scale units.

(xii) Amount due to small scale units does not affect interrelationship of small scale units with large ones. The lower the amount due, the higher would be the degree of interrelationship.

5.7 OPERATIONAL DEFINITION OF CONCEPTS

(i) Interrelationship : Interrelationship means mutual or reciprocal relations. In this study interrelationship means mutual relations between small and large scale units.

The mutual relationship will be reflected in the help rendered by the large scale units to the small scale units. The various types of help rendered are giving job work with or without material, selling of old machines at concessional rates, supply of tools and accessories, provision of engineering service, giving transport facilities and giving drawings and samples.

(ii) Small Scale Unit : Any engineering unit with an investment in plant and machinery not exceeding Rs. 15 lakhs and supplying accessories or components or both to large scale engineering units situated in Coimbatore region. Sometimes they have been referred to as small units.

(iii) Large Scale Units : Any engineering unit having investment in plant and machinery exceeding Rs. 15 lakhs and depending on small scale units for accessories or components or both.

(iv) Engineering Unit : Any unit manufacturing textile machinery, pumpsets, diesel engines, motors, agricultural implements and lathe and accessories or components or both for the above categories of machines is called as engineering unit.

(v) Technical Qualification of Small Entrepreneurs : Technical qualification includes Industrial Training Institute Certificate and Diploma and Degree in Engineering.

(vi) Previous Employment of Small Entrepreneurs : Small entrepreneurs of the sample units who have been employed in large engineering units selected for the study in the capacity as worker, supervisor, office assistant and executive.

(vii) Standard Products : The small scale units located within 5 kilometres radius of the large scale counterparts have been categorised as units near the large scale units. Any small scale units located beyond 5 kilometres from their respective large scale units have been categorised as units far away.

(viii) Standard Products : Standard products are products for which there are continuous orders from large scale units.

(ix) Non-Standard Products : Non-standard products are products for which there are no continuous orders or order may be for different products every time.

(x) Period of Contact : This is calculated from the date on which each small scale unit is getting orders from the large scale unit up to 31st March 1980.

(xi) Communal Identity : This term means entrepreneurs of small and large scale units belonging to the same community.

(xii) Personal Interaction : This term means the personal relationship between the entrepreneurs of small and large scale units. This relationship is due to their past relationship as members of school/college peer groups.

(xiii) Social Relationship : This means the relationship between the entrepreneurs of small scale units and executives of large scale units. The relationship is created through attending marriages, dinners, religious functions, making courtesy calls and the like.

(xiv) Training Facility : This means Apprenticeship Training imparted by large scale units.

(xv) Certificate of Order : The large scale units give a certificate stating the quantum of order given to small scale units. This enables the small scale units to borrow funds from financial institutions.

(xvi) Engineering Service : This means that the small scale units receive personal engineering service from large scale units in the manufacture of the product.

(xvii) Drawings : Drawing means the sketch of accessories and components. This large scale units give the drawings to the small scale units.

(xviii) Entrepreneur : One who takes the ultimate responsibility for management of small and large scale units is called the entrepreneur.

(xix) Small Entrepreneur : Entrepreneurs of small scale engineering units.

5.8 METHODOLOGY AND TOOLS

This study is an empirical research based on the survey method. First hand data were collected from the field directly and from the records of the selected institutions through interview schedule and mailed questionnaire.

The interrelationship of small scale units with large scale units has involved a survey of selected small and large scale engineering units situated in Coimbatore region.

Data relating to small scale engineering units have been collected through personal interview. For this purpose an interview schedule has been used.

Data with regard to the benefits of interrelationship accruing to small scale units have been collected from each sample small scale unit through a mailed questionnaire.

A number of discussions have been held with well-informed persons such as industrialists, government officials and managers employed in engineering units.

5.9 CONSTRUCTION OF TOOLS AND PRE-TEST

Interview schedule and questionnaire used in this study have been structured by the researcher himself. The variables to be studied have been identified in the preliminary interview with some selected small scale industrialists and officials of large engineering units. The researcher interviewed 9 small industrialists, 3 from Chinniampalayam, 2 from Peelamedu, 2 from Ganapathy and 2 from Madukkarai (all being the industrial pockets of Coimbatore District). He also had a discussion with the General Manager ELGI Equipments Limited Coimbatore, Production Manager Textool Company Limited Coimbatore and the Planning Engineer, PSG Industrial Institute Coimbatore to identify the variables.

The variables thus identified by the researcher have been operationalised. The schedule and questionnaire so drafted were circulated among a few research workers for a critical review with regard to wording, format, sequence and the like. They were redrafted in the light of their comments.

Interview schedule for the small scale units has been in English. The questionnaire for small scale units has been administered in the vernacular.

A pilot study was conducted in August-October 1979 and the schedule and questionnaires have been pre-tested and revised.

5.10 SAMPLING DESIGN

Coimbatore region has been selected for the study for two reasons. The first is the predominance of Coimbatore in engineering industry which is highly responsible for the industrial pre-eminence of Tamil Nadu. Secondly the researcher has observed a network of small scale units catering to the needs of large scale engineering units in the area in and around Coimbatore City.

5.11 GEOGRAPHICAL COVERAGE

The study covers the area included in the city of Coimbatore and other belt areas such as Chinniampalayam, Goundenpalayam, Parianaickanpalayam, Podanur, Kuniamuthur, Madukkarai and Sunderapuram.

5.12 PERIOD OF COVERAGE

Data relating to four years 1974-75 to 1978-79 have been collected from the small scale units.

5.13 FIELD WORK AND COLLECTION OF DATA

Field work for this study was carried out by the researcher himself. It was conducted during the period from November 1979 to September 1980 covering a period of 11 months.

The researcher has used interview schedule for collecting data from small engineering units and collected data fixing prior appointment with interviews.

After collecting the information through the interview schedule, the questionnaire for small scale units has been mailed with a self-addressed envelope. Completed schedules and questionnaires have been checked and edited. the omissions and commissions have been rectified by revisits to the field and by correspondence.

5.14 DATA PROCESSING

After completing the schedule and questionnaires, a thorough check up of the data has been made. The missing details have been collected by revisits and correspondence. Afterwards, editing of the data has been done.

For further processing, the data have been transcribed on transcription cards.

5.15 MEASUREMENT OF VARIABLES AND CONSTRUCTION OF SCALE

The main theme of this study is the interrelationship of small scale engineering units with large scale units. With a view to applying statistical methods such as Analysis of Variance, Chi-Square Test and 't' tests, scaling technique has been used for measuring variables. There have been two types of variables in the study — dependent and independent variables.

The dependent variable of the study is "interrelationship". This has been measured through a scale by name "Interrelationship Scale". The scale has been based on a scoring scheme constructed with eight components such as buying old machines at concessional rate, getting job work with material, getting tools, receiving engineering service, availing transport facility, getting drawings, getting samples, and job order without material. The scale is similar to the one developed in the thesis "A Study of Agro-Industrial Integration in Perianaickenpalayam Community Development Block of Coimbatore District," submitted to the Karnataka University in 1976.

TABLE 1

Sample Small Scale Units Covered by the Study

Sl. No.	*Name of large scale units selected for the study*	*Number of small scale units depending on large scale units*	*Number of small scale units selected for the study*
1.	PSG Industrial Institutes	51	15
2.	Lakshmi Machine Works Limited	40	12
3.	ELGI Equipments Limited	25	7
4.	Textools Company Limited	22	6
5.	Coimbatore Machine Tools	7	2
6.	Madras Machine Tools Limited	5	2
7.	Everest Engineering Works	4	1
	Total	154	45

The independent variables which influence the dependent variable of the study are the following:

(i) Technical qualification of small entrepreneurs;

(ii) Previous employment of small entrepreneurs;

(iii) Nearness to large scale units;

(iv) Nature of products of small scale units;

(v) Period of relationship between small and large scale units;

(vi) Communal identity of entrepreneurs of small and large scale units;

(vii) Personal interaction of entrepreneurs of small scale units with that of large ones through school/college peer groups;

(viii) Social relationship of small entrepreneurs with the executives of large scale units;

(ix) Training facilities made available in large scale units for the employees of small scale units;

(x) Erstwhile employees of small scale units employed in large scale units;

(xi) Issue of certificate of order by large scale units to the entrepreneurs of small scale units;

(xii) Amount due to small scale units from large scale units.

The above variables have been categorised.

The benefits of interrelationship accruing to small scale units have been measured with the help of mean benefit score.

5.16 FRAMEWORK OF ANALYSIS

The analysis of the study is as follows: First the extent and variation of interrelationship of small scale units with large scale units has been measured through the scale called 'interrelationship scale', constructed on the basis of eight components. They are :

(i) Buying old machines at concessional rate;

(ii) Getting job work with material;

(iii) Getting tools;

(iv) Receiving engineering service;

(v) Availing of transport facility;

(vi) Getting drawings;

(vii) Getting samples;

(viii) Job order without materials.

These eight components have been quantified with the help of a scoring scheme.

Secondly, twelve factors promoting interrelationship of small scale units with large scale units have been categorised. The influence of independent variables (factors) on the dependent variable (interrelationship) has been analysed with the help of measures of Central Tendency, Percentages, Analysis of Variance, 't' test and 'Chi-Square' test.

Finally benefits of interrelationship accruing to small scale units have been measured, through the mean benefit scores. Twelve benefits have been identified in this study. For each benefit of interrelationship, the mean score of medium interrelationship units and low interrelationship units have been found out separately by applying the scoring schemes. The mean scores of medium inter-relationship units are compared with those of low interrelationship units. This comparison has been done separately for all these 12 benefits of interrelationship.

5.17 SCHEME OF THE REPORT

The report has been organised into eight chapters.

The first chapter discusses the introduction and design of the study. It covers introduction, statement of the problem, review of previous studies, scope of the study, objectives of the study, hypothesis, operational definition of concepts, methodology and tools, construction of tools and pre-test, sampling design, geographical coverage, period of coverage, field work and collection of data, data processing, measurement of variables and construction of scale, framework of analysis and scheme of the report.

The second chapter discusses the concept of interrelationship.

The third chapter deals with the progress of small scale units in Coimbatore District and Tamil Nadu with special reference to engineering industry.

The fourth chapter presents a general appraisal of sample small scale units.

The fifth chapter presents the extent and variation of interrelationship. This chapter contains four parts. Part A deals with general approach to interrelationship. Part B discusses the measure of interrelationship between small and large scale units. Part C presents the extent and variation of interrelationship by components and Part D presents the extent and variation of interrelationship among the small scale units in Coimbatore region.

The Sixth chapter analyses the factors influencing interrelationship of small scale units with large scale units. For each factor a theoretical background, Averages, Analysis of variance, 't' test and Chi-Square Test have been presented in this chapter.

The seventh chapter deals with the benefits of interrelationship with large scale units accruing to small scale units. For each benefit the mean scores for low and medium interrelationship units have been presented.

The last chapter presents the summary of the findings and suggestions for achieving higher degree of interrelationship.

REFERENCES

1 Design of the Ph.D thesis titled "Small Scale Engineering Industry in Coimbatore Region — A Study of Interrelationship with Large Scale Industry" submitted to the University of Madras for the award of Ph.D. Degree.

CHAPTER THREE

METHODS OF INVESTIGATION

1. *Survey Method of Investigation*
2. *Case Study Method of Investigation*
3. *Experimental Method of Investigation*
4. *Scientific Method of Business Research*

1. SURVEY METHOD OF INVESTIGATION

A social survey has been defined as a "fact-finding study dealing chiefly with working - class poverty and with the nature and problems of the community."[1] The discovery of fact is the essential feature of a survey. The fact may be related to poverty, town-planning, market research, unemployment problem and housing problem and the like.

1.1 PURPOSE OF SURVEYS

A desk research aims at theoretical dissertation. A social survey is a field-oriented study. The purposes of surveys are the following.

(i) The main purpose of a survey is to provide someone with information. A business concern interested in finding out what detergents a particular segment of people are using, conducts a survey and finds out the fact. The survey of this type is only descriptive in nature.

(ii) Another important purpose of survey is to explain rather than to describe. A study for the purpose of assessing the influence of various factors upon some phenomenon is called a 'casual' survey. For example, a researcher conducts a sur-

vey for identifying the various reasons for overdues in Primary Co-operative Credit Societies. This survey only explains the various factors responsible for huge overdues.

(iii) Surveys provide information for the formulation of hypotheses. A pilot survey can be conducted to collect data and with the help of these data hypotheses can be formulated. These hypotheses can be tested by further investigation. Thus, surveys enable the researcher to formulate hypotheses and test the hypotheses.

(iv) Social survey offers scope for the collection of primary data relating to social problems through interview schedules, questionnaires and checklists.

1.2 SUBJECT MATTER OF SOCIAL SURVEYS

Moser, C.A. has divided the subject matter of surveys into four broad classes.[2]

(i) The demographic characteristics of a set of people;

(ii) Their social environment;

(iii) Their social activities;

(iv) Their opinion and attitudes.

The demographic characteristics of people include factors such as family composition, marital status, fertility, age, family income, number of dependents and the like.

The social environment covers all the social factors including occupation, housing conditions and social amenities. These factors are very important because a number of social actions are conditioned by the environment in which people live.

Social activities of people include the use of leisure, travelling habits, expenditure patterns, television viewing, radio-listening and newspaper reading.

Opinions and attitudes include data regarding the level of information, opinion and attitude of the people towards various social factors and the motives and expectations of the people.

1.3 TYPES OF SURVEY

Surveys are conducted by various agencies for various purposes. On the basis of the subject matter, techniques of data collection and the agencies, surveys may be classified as follows :

1.3.1 GENERAL OR SPECIFIC SURVEYS

When a survey is conducted for collecting general information without any particular object, it is known as a general survey. For example, the census of population which has normally been carried out every ten years is a general survey.

Specific surveys are conducted for a specific problem. Inadequate housing causes more widespread distress than any other social problem. A survey regarding the housing problem is called specific survey.

1.3.2 REGULAR AND AD HOC SURVEYS

Some surveys are regular in nature and must be repeated after regular intervals. For undertaking such survey a permanent machinery for collecting information has to be set up. For example, every year a pre-budget economic survey is undertaken by the Ministry of Finance.

Ad hoc surveys are undertaken mostly for testing hypotheses. The sociologist must not collect facts until he has a hypotheses. For the formulation of hypotheses surveys are undertaken. Surveys will also enable us to put the hypotheses to test.

1.3.3 GOVERNMENT SOCIAL SURVEY

The Government undertakes the survey through the Central Statistical Organisation, Department of Statistics and Ministry of Planning, Government of India. They provide data on different sectors of the Indian economy.

1.4 PLANNING A SOCIAL SURVEY

The planning of a social survey is a combination of technical and organisational decisions. The decision regarding the following must be taken before the execution of the survey :

1.4.1 PURPOSE OF THE SURVEY

The first task of planning is to lay down the survey's purpose precisely. The purpose of the survey helps the surveyors to form a clear view and it leads to more efficient enquiry. Failure to lay down the purpose will undermine the quality of the survey.

1.4.2 COVERAGE

Decide the population to be covered and determine the method of selecting the respondents. Determine the type of sample to be used. Then prepare the sampling frame and size of the sample to impart desired accuracy. Effective provision should be made for dealing with non-response.

1.4.3 COLLECTION OF DATA

The choice of the method of collecting data depends upon the unit of enquiry (individual, household etc.). A study of crowd behaviour would call for observational techniques. For an enquiry among an educated section of the population, a mailed questionnaire might be adequate. A survey of general population entailing many complicated questions would call for personal interviewing. Each method has its advantages and disadvantages.

1.4.4 ERRORS

Every stage of the survey process is a potential source of error. Inaccuracies may enter, through interviewing, editing, coding, tabulating and analysis. There is the risk of memory errors, sampling errors and non-sampling errors. In planning a survey one must anticipate the source of errors and take necessary precautions.

1.4.5 FIELDWORK

The quality of the survey largely depends upon the type of interviewers and the method of selecting them. Every organisation (researcher) must establish a policy on the following questions.

(i) Recruitment of field staff-full-time or part-time.

(ii) Method of supervision of field staff.

(iii) Checks to be made on the honesty of the staff. It must be decided either on the basis of piece rate or time rate or equal payment or unequal payment.

1.4.6 PROCESSING AND ANALYSIS

When the questionnaires come in, the omissions and commissions must be checked. Finally comes the analysis, the interpretation of results and the preparation of the report.

The methods of analysis should be given careful consideration at the planning stage. If a computer is to be employed, the code lists should be checked to ensure that they meet the programmes to be employed.

1.4.7 DOCUMENTS

Questionnaires, interview schedules, check lists, record cards and time and expenses sheets must be prepared.

1.4.8 TIMING, COST AND STAFFING

Decide the time within which the results are needed. Once the date is fixed, a schedule for the completion of the survey at various stages must be set up.

An estimate of the cost of printing the documents, selection of the sample, fieldwork, mailing, processing and tabulating, preparation of the report and overheads must be made.

In social research surveys, the skills of various experts like sociologists, psychologists, statisticians and the computer specialists are needed. These experts will have to be engaged at various stages of the survey.

1.5 PILOT SURVEYS

A pilot survey is a small scale replica of the main survey. The pilot survey is a dress rehearsal. The pilot study provides guidance on the following :

(i) The adequacy of the sampling frame to be followed for the survey.

(ii) The pilot study enables the researcher to acquire prior knowledge about the population to be sampled.

(iii) The probable number of refusals and non-contacts can be roughly be estimated from the pilot survey. As a result a particular data collection method may be chosen in preference to others.

(iv) After examining the alternative methods such as observation, questionnaire and interview schedule the suitability of the method of collecting the data can be found out from the pilot study.

(v) The pilot study provides scope to find out whether the wording in the questionnaire is simple, clear, unambiguous or free from technical terms.

(vi) The pilot study enables to test the efficiency of the instructions and general briefing of interviews. Sometimes the instructions may be adequate, but the interviewer may be doing a poor job.

(vii) The pilot study provides training to the interviewers.

(viii) The probable cost and duration of the main survey and its various stages will be known with the help of the pilot study. Pilot survey is valuable if the main survey is too long and too expensive.

The size and design of the pilot survey is a matter of convenience. The sample should be of comparable structure of that of main survey. The sample of the pilot survey must be widespread as the main sample. If two forms of questions are to be compared, each should be tried out. All the techniques of processing and analysis of data have to be piloted.

1.6 MERITS OF SURVEY METHOD

The survey method has the following merits.

(i) The survey method enables the researcher to come into direct contact with the people whom he wants to study.

(ii) The survey provides scope for the introduction of a new theory. For example, a long time poverty was the cause for

crime. But the surveys conducted in advanced countries have falsified this theory.

(iii) A survey facilitates the researcher to observe the emotional impact of social situation. The survey method is well suited to study the people with specialised characteristics.

(iv) Surveys are conducted for business purposes. For example, to ascertain the popularity of the products introduced by a business concern.

(v) Survey is meant to provide information regarding practical problems.

(vi) Survey is conducted to investigate some cause and effect relationship.

1.7 LIMITATIONS OF SURVEY METHOD

(i) Most of the surveys are conducted on sample basis, and the informant may not become the representative of the universe.

(ii) Survey method lays importance upon current problems. A comprehensive study of the society is not possible.

(iii) Survey method refers to study undertaken for short time. A study involving long term development cannot be undertaken under this method.

(iv) A survey method of research requires a considerable amount of money for printing of schedules for fieldwork, training and supervision, tabulation and analysis of the data.

(v) Most of the surveys are conducted in a hurry and the reliability and validity of such information is questionable.

(vi) A survey will lead to desired result, if the survey has been perfectly pre-planned. But a perfect pre-planning is seldom possible.

1.8 SOCIAL SURVEYS IN INDIA

In India a number of socio-economic surveys were initiated by individuals and institutions.

In 1913 a sociological and statistical survey of some Madras villages was undertaken by Sir Theodore Morison.

Dr. Gilbert Slater and Dr.H.H. Mann in 1916 undertook a socio-economic survey of Madras and Bombay provinces.

Dr. Mann in 1918 undertook a socio-economic survey of Poona.

The Indian Statistical Institute has conducted surveys such as Consumer Preference in Calcutta, Bengal Handloom Survey, the surveys of Rural Indebtedness and Agricultural labour and the National Sample Survey.

The Reserve Bank of India's All India Rural Credit Survey headed by Thiru. A.D. Gorwala in 1951 aimed at studying the pattern of agricultural credit in different parts of the country is a landmark in the field of co-operative banking.

An outstanding development in the country was the setting up of the National Council of Applied Economic Research (NCAER), New Delhi. The NCAER has initiated a series of national and regional studies on several facets of human life.

The University Grants Commission (UGC) and Indian Council of Social Science Research (ICSSR) have come in a big way to provide funds to undertake social science research. In addition to these agencies, the foreign agencies like Ford Foundation and Rockfeller Foundation have been providing financial assistance to conduct social research. Many private foundations established by Tatas, Birlas and many other industrial and business families and companies promote social science research in a laudable way.

2. CASE STUDY METHOD OF INVESTIGATION

Case study is an important tool of social investigation. It has been used extensively in Psychology, Education, Sociology, Economics and Political Science. It has been used for tracing the evolution and growth of a social problem. A particular unit can be investigated intensively with the help of the case study method.

According to Pauline V. Young, case study is a method of exploring and analysing the life of a social unit. The social unit may be a person, family, community or an institution.

In social research the term 'case' refers to a unit of study. The unit may be a person, group of persons, institution, or community. Each case is unique. Therefore a case is non-comparable and it yields non-additive and non-quantitative data. The quantitative methods are not suitable because they fail to take into account the unique features of the case.

2.1 EVOLUTION OF CASE STUDY METHOD

Frederic Le Play (1806-1882) in the continent and Charles Booth (1840-1916) in England may be described as the fathers of the social survey method. From survey method in due course sprang the case study method of modern times. Le Play a social reformer and an economist worked on the case studies on "European Workers' Standard of Living," in 1855. The features of his studies are the following :

(i) The family was the basic unit of study.

(ii) Le Play was in constant contact with the selected families.

(iii) He measured the diverse components of family life.

Charles Booth the author of a monumental study, "Life and Labour of the People of London", adopted the case study method. He chose to live inconspicuously among the poor of East End of London and was a participant observer. He studied the economic and social conditions of the whole population of London. His famous study led to the amelioration of the conditions of the poor in London.

The followers of Le Play and Booth have contributed to the growth of literature as well as progressive refinement of methodology of case study.

The Research Programme Committee of the Planning Commission sponsored a large number of case studies in 1950 in India. The Economic Survey of Madras City, Beggar Surveys in Hyderabad, Prostitution Survey in Bombay and Industrial case studies in Madras State are some of the notable case studies undertaken in India.

It is erroneous to think that after the advent of highly sophisticated techniques, case studies are on the wane. Even today the case study is popular in India and foreign countries.

2.2 CHARACTERISTICS OF CASE STUDY METHOD

(i) The case study method aims at deep and detailed study of the unit.

(ii) It is a comprehensive study. It covers a wide span of time.

(iii) The number of units may vary from single unit to a few dozen or even a few hundreds. They are not selected according to some scientific techniques of sampling.

(iv) The researcher has to rely on his own power of observation and sense of logic than on the facts.

(v) A greater part of man's life is subjective, unknown and incapable of observation. The understanding of human nature and his actions requires much deeper probe and a keen insight. For such indepth study case study method is ideally suitable.

2.3 SOURCES OF DATA

In case study, the information may be collected from various sources. Case studies are not limited to any single source of data collection. They command a number of sources. The important sources of data are the following :

(i) Life histories.
(ii) Personal records.
(iii) Personal documents.
(iv) Personal letters.
(v) Confessions.
(vi) Biographies.
(vii) Interviewing individuals.
(viii) Observation.

The above sources include the use of written materials about the respondent and the collection of data through interview and observation. If the study is pertaining to life history of a person, the entire range of information from his childhood to old age is thoroughly authenticated and tested. Every aspect of his life is taken into consideration.

2.4 STEPS INVOLVED IN CASE STUDY

The various steps involved in a case study are as follows :

2.4.1 CHOICE OF CASES

The researcher has to decide which unit has to be taken for study. The case may be general or specific. The researcher has to choose either of the two.

2.4.2 IDENTIFICATION OF THE UNIT

The unit of study may be an individual or a group of persons or an institution or a group of institutions.

2.4.3 NUMBER OF CASES

We can obtain the results easily if the cases are few. If the results are generalised on the basis of few number of cases the result will be biased or wrong.

2.4.4 COLLECTION OF DATA

The researcher should use different techniques and tools to collect data about different aspects of the unit. The study of personal documents, life histories, observations, interviews, questionnaires, schedules, a variety of tests like intelligence tests, achievement tests and aptitude tests are certain techniques adopted in case study for gathering data. The collected data should be recorded properly.

2.4.5 ANALYSIS OF FACTORS

All collected data are integrated and analysed. The most dominant, less dominant and neutral elements should be discriminated.

2.4.6 INTERPRETATION AND REPORTING OF DATA

The facts collected have to be classified and analysed. Afterwards, the facts must be explained and interpreted. The interpretation must be in logical and convenient form.

The findings have to be adequately reported in order to make them more valuable to the public. In reporting, the researcher has to present the problem investigated, the research methods employed, the results and the conclusions arrived at as a result of the investigation. The report must be such that the reader can easily understand, assess and verify the validity of the conclusions.

2.5 ADVANTAGES OF CASE STUDY

The following are some of the specific advantages of the case study.

(i) A case study helps to probe the entire life span of a social unit in depth. For example, the case study of PSG and Sons Charities, Coimbatore will enable the researcher to bring to limelight the unknown factors responsible for the growth of the charities and its role in the development of Coimbatore as an industrial centre.

(ii) The case study method lays a greater stress upon the emotional side of social phenomena. In order to study a social phenomenon, the activities of men or even a group have to be studied in depth. For such type of study case study method is ideally suitable.

(iii) A variety of habits, traits and qualities are combined in a social unit and a case study enables the study of all these characteristics.

(iv) Case data are useful to pure research and they provide clues for further research.

(v) Case study is also useful for the formulation of hypothesis which will lead to further research.

2.6 LIMITATIONS OF CASE STUDY

(i) It is very difficult to draw generalisations after studying a few cases. The results of case study are not applicable to the universe.

(ii) There is a vast scope for errors which arise due to faulty selection of a case, inaccurate observation and erroneous reporting.

(iii) Case study is loose and unsystematic and incapable of verification and generalization.

(iv) There is a temptation to ignore research design and hence the study is not systematic.

(v) It is costly, time consuming and wasteful in certain cases where the objectives are limited.

3. EXPERIMENTAL METHOD OF INVESTIGATION

Most of the researches are conducted in the field of Physical Science through the experimental method. Gradually the experimental method has been finding favour with social sciences such as Psychology, Sociology and Education.

3.1 WHAT IS EXPERIMENTATION?

Experimentation is a special type of investigation used to determine whether and in what manner variables are related to each other. The Experimentation is concerned with determining whether there is a relationship between an independent variable (IV) and dependent variable (DV).[2] A researcher has observed that heavy smokers suffer from illness and have a higher rate of death than non-smokers. Those who challenge this, argue that the genetic factor could be causing both desire to smoke and the illness.

Now the researcher is concerned with determining whether there is a relationship between an independent variable (IV) and dependent variable (DV). Here smoking is taken as an independent variable and illness as an independent variable. The experiment can be done in such a way that the researcher takes some cases and finds illness in the case of smokers and no illness in the case of non-smokers. As the genetic factors influence the illness, the researcher has to create conditions so that these factors are not allowed to affect illness. This idealised concept can be implemented in laboratory conditions.

3.2 TYPES OF EXPERIMENTS

Greenwood in his book, *Experimental Sociology* has mentioned the following five types of experiments. They are :

3.2.1 TRIAL AND ERROR EXPERIMENT

Under this experiment the researcher does not prepare a structural plan of study. The researcher prepares hypotheses and tests them on social conditions. He may test with a small group but enlarge it. The techniques of this experiment undergo a lot of changes.

3.2.2 CONTROLLED OBSERVATIONAL STUDY

This is a laboratory type of experiment. The subject to be observed is kept under controlled conditions and changes in it are observed.

3.2.3 FIELD EXPERIMENT

It is also called as natural experiment, but it is different from field study. In the case of field study the researcher observes the phenomena without any kind of manipulation. But in the case of field experiment, the researcher manipulates the independent variable. Natural experiment is highly useful to study the effect of advertising on sales, training methods on productivity and so on. For example, an experimenter wanted to measure the price elasticity of demand for four different products. The products were placed in 16 different stores and prices were recorded. It has been found out that for Product A, 1 per cent change in price has brought about 1.5n per cent change in sales volume. But for Product B there is only 1.27 per cent change in sales volume, for Product C 1.58 per cent and for Product D 1.74 per cent.

3.2.4 EX-POST-FACTOR EXPERIMENT

In the evaluation of the effectiveness of the development projects, this method has been followed. With a view to evaluating the benefits derived by the farmers from Cauvery Dam constructed by the Government of Tamil Nadu, the income derived by the farmers after the construction of the project can be compared with the income of the farmers at the time of installation of the project.

3.2.5 LABORATORY EXPERIMENT

Laboratory experiment has been used in the filed of Market Research. For example, an experimenter wanted to measure the price elasticity of demand for four different products. In the laboratory experiment an artificial 'store' was set up and the home markets were asked to go through the store and select products as if on a regular shopping trip. Prices were varied. For Product A, a 1 per cent change in price has brought about 1.25 per cent change in sales volume, for Product B 0.64 per cent, for Product C 0.76 per cent and for Product D 1.14 per cent.

3.3 PLANNING THE EXPERIMENT

Planning the experiment is very important before conducting the experiment. The following steps must be followed in conducting the experiment.

3.3.1 SELECTION OF THE PROBLEM

The experimenter has to identify the problem of experiment. He has to search for the variables which affect the phenomena. All the problems cannot be studied by experimental method. But all problems which can be studied by experimental method can also be studied by non-experimental methods. The result of non-experimental methods are not clear or useful.

3.3.2 SELECTION OF THE SETTING

The researcher has to select the setting of the experiment. For example, an experimenter wants to study the effect of workers' participation in management. He must select an organisation, where the workers participate in management decision process. Moreover, he must have free access to the data and also freedom to publish the data.

3.3.3 RESEARCH DESIGN

The research design is a structured plan prepared before undertaking the experiment. The design will explain the manner in which the experiment is to be done. It also offers guidelines for manipulating the situations. In a prolonged experiment, it is not possible to have a design.

3.3.4 PILOT STUDY

The pilot study enables the experimenter to measure the extent of co-operation he will get from the person under investigation. He can identify the causation factors which influence the phenomenon to be studied. The plan of experiment prepared prior to the pilot study can be revised in the light of the experience gained through the pilot study.

3.4 MERITS OF EXPERIMENTAL METHOD

The experimental method has the following advantages.

(i) It permits the determination of cause and effect relationship more clearly than any other method of investigation. If a researcher wants to study the extent of relationship between higher wages and higher output, the experiment method is highly suitable.

(ii) The variable under study is manipulated leaving others unchanged. We can locate with precision the effect of varying degrees of stimulus.

(iii) Experiment method is the best method for testing a hypothesis. Testing of hypothesis requires a study of relationship between variables under varied conditions.

Experimenters create artificial situations so that they can obtain the particular data needed. The experiments are artificial in the sense that situations are usually created for testing purposes. This artificiality is the essence of the experimental method, since it gives researchers more control over the factors they are studying.

(iv) Experimental research is widely used in Marketing. When new products are developed, they are tested and retested in many technical experiments before the final models are

determined. Months or even years are spent in experimental work of this type.

3.5 ADMINISTRATIVE PROBLEMS OF EXPERIMENTATION

Many administrative problems are to be encountered in conducting experiments. They are the following:

(i) Frequently co-operation must be obtained from the individual under investigation and from those persons who are in charge of setting up of the experiment.

(ii) For a successful experiment it is necessary that all causative factors except the one under study must be strictly unchanged. But the social phenomenon is affected by a number of causes producing various influences at times in different directions. Then it is very difficult to control them.

(iii) Competitive circumstances may create difficult experimental conditions. If a new product is tested in the market, competitors will become aware of the test. They will be abreast of new developments. If the results of the tests are measured in sales, the competitor may be able to learn as much from the test as the experimenter at less expenses.

(iv) True experimentation cannot take place without hypothesis. Such hypotheses are usually developed from underlying theory and such theory is developed from extensive observation and description. For example, in market research little theory is now available.

4. SCIENTIFIC METHOD OF BUSINESS RESEARCH

The scientific method is systematic procedure of formulating a problem, measuring occurrences and testing the hypotheses concerning those occurrences.

In the humanities, consisting of history and languages experimentation is not often feasible. The historical method is often followed and hence experimentation with hypotheses is not possible. In Sociology and Psychology the behaviour of human beings is the chief object of the study. Since the human behaviour is not subject to close control, scientific method is not followed. As the field of business activity is usually classified as a social science, a more detailed discussion of the social sciences related to the scientific method follows.

The findings of research in the field of physical sciences are exact. In social science research there is difficulty of carrying on experiments under controlled conditions. There are II steps involved in making the social science, scientific. They are :

4.1 BECOME AWARE THAT A PROBLEM EXISTS

The manager of a business must be aware of a problem and must be willing to admit that a difficulty exists. Problems may sometimes relate to questions whether an activity can be improved or new opportunities developed for increasing the net income of the business.

4.2 DEFINE THE PROBLEM AND PURPOSES OF THE RESEARCH PROJECT

What exactly is the difficulty? What is the future of the problem? Is the problem serious? How many parts of the problem are involved? Is the problem serious? The definition of the problem should also include a detailed consideration of the possible uses to which the results are to be put.

4.3 SET FORTH HYPOTHESES

This step requires that careful guesses should be made as the possible causes or solutions of the problem. In this the experience and knowledge about the business are highly useful provided he does not permit bias. A fertile mind could recall possible cause and effect relationship.

4.4 DETERMINE WHAT INFORMATION WILL BE REQUIRED

The definition of the problem, the possible uses to which the results are to be put as well as the hypotheses that are set forth, all help to determine the exact nature of information that must be obtained.

4.5 DECIDE THE METHODS TO BE USED FOR COLLECTING INFORMATION

Efficient methods that will obtain the necessary information with minimum of expenditure of time, money and personnel must be used.

The data collection techniques are :

- *(i)* Published material.
- *(ii)* Unpublished material.
- *(iii)* Survey techniques.
- *(iv)* Observation.
- *(v)* Experimentation.

4.6 COLLECTION OF INFORMATION OR EVIDENCE

Careful management and control of research personnel, materials and devices used will bring more accurate results as well as save time and money.

4.7 A COMPILE FINDINGS IN SYSTEMATIC FORM

The factual findings must be prepared in a clear and concise manner and the findings are significant to the project under study.

4.8 ANALYSE FINDINGS TO DETERMINE WHETHER THEY SUBSTAINTIATE OR ELIMINATE HYPOTHESES

It may involve testing the hypotheses by statistical techniques. The exact significance of the findings must be determined and too much or too little of them may prejudice the findings.

4.9 WRITE THE FINAL REPORT BRINGING OUT THE FULL SIGNIFICANCE OF FINDINGS AND ANY INDICATED CONCLUSIONS

The nature of the problem and the purposes of the project must always be kept in mind. The length and complexity will depend on the nature of the research project.

4.10 MAKE SPECIFIC RECOMMENDATIONS

Every recommendation will be based on the facts obtained in the research process. The reasoning followed must lead to logical, unquestionable conclusions fully documented by material contained in the findings of the project.

4.11 FOLLOW UP

The follow up is important for three reasons :

(i) Unless research results are carefully considered and acted upon the project will be useless;

(ii) As a part of follow-up the researcher will be available for any explanation needed; and

(iii) The results of the application of the research findings in actual practice can be studied.

REFERENCES

1. Sir Claus Moser and G. Kalton, Survey Methods in Social Investigation, Heinemann Educational Books Ltd., 1974, p.1.

2. *Ibid.*, p.2.

CHAPTER FOUR

METHODS OF COLLECTING PRIMARY DATA

1. OBSERVATION

Observation is the basic method of obtaining information about the world around us. All observations are not scientific observations. An observation becomes scientific, if it is planned and recorded systematically and is subject to checks and controls on validity and reliability.

1.1 TYPES OF OBSERVATION

Observation may take place either in real life setting or in laboratory. The observer may participate in the group he is observing or he may be an observer from outside. His presence may be unknown to the people he is observing.

The scientific observation may be broadly classified as under :

Structured/unstructured observation.

Participant/non-participant/disguised observation.

The choice of an observational technique depends upon the study. In the exploratory study the observer is participating in group activity.

For the experimental type, the observation procedure is structured and it involves a minimum of participation on the part of the observer.

Now let us discuss the major types of observational procedures.

1.1.1 STRUCTURED OBSERVATION

The investigator should decide the data he needs. Sound recordings and motion pictures have been used to describe the overall nature of the event or to code certain actions of a member. Motion pictures, tape recording and television may be very helpful in presenting a overall view of a social event.

1.1.2 UNSTRUCTURED OBSERVATION

There is no careful definition of the units to be observed and the information to be recorded. Any record of the information may affect the naturalness of the situation and create suspicion in the minds of persons being observed. With a view to overcome these problems, different observers observe same event and record the information. This enables the observers to maintain accuracy and avoids the getting of facts by one or few observers.

1.1.3 PARTICIPANT OBSERVATION

The observer is sharing to a greater or lesser degree the life of the group he is observing. The members of the groups are unaware of the researcher's purpose. The researcher obtains a greater depth of experience. He can also check the truth of statements made by the members of the group.

1.1.4 NON-PARTICIPANT OBSERVATION

The observer is not sharing to a greater or lesser degree the life of the group he is observing. A sociologist can become a criminal in order to study the behaviour of a criminal gang.

1.2 AIDS IN THE FIELDS OF OBSERVATION

A number of devices are used as aids in the field of observation. A brief discussion of these aids is attempted.

1.2.1 DETAILED FIELD NOTES

The field notes taken at the time of observation are carefully transcribed as soon as possible after observation.

1.2.2 PHOTOGRAPHS

They tend to present accurately a mass of details. The photographic eye views with authenticity and impartiality. It has no preconceived notions and selective interests. It is difficult to depict the facial expression and particularly the expression of the eyes by any other means. At times words can be deficient in expressing the hunger of children, despair of refugees and so on. In such cases photographs are highly useful.

1.2.3 MAPS

The social background of the respondents can be known from the maps. The social base maps show the relationship of topographical aspects of a community to its social organisation. This will facilitate further study.

1.2.4 SCHEDULE

They help in standardising the recording of observed phenomenon. They isolate individual elements and thus facilitate concentration and measurement.

1.2.5 SOCIOMETRIC SCALES

They are used in the measurement of social attitudes, moral status, home environment, social press judgement, participation and variety of other factors.

1.2.6 BEHAVIOUR DIARIES

This is mainly meant for recording the exceptional behaviour of an individual as observed by the researcher over a period of time. This method is time consuming and its effectiveness depends upon the skill of the observer in determining what incidents to be recorded.

1.2.7 PERIODIC SUMMARIES

The researcher makes periodic summaries of behaviour instead of recording his observations after or during each group session. He records his general impression of the behaviour of the individuals.

1.2.8 CHECKLISTS

The observer would merely check the occurrence of the indicated habits or skills of an individual. He merely discovers the frequency with which they are demonstrated by the individuals under observation.

1.3 BASIC PRINCIPLES APPLICABLE TO OBSERVATION

1. The problem should be formulated and specific points needing investigation should be decided.
2. Devise a method of recording the results.
3. Observe carefully and critically.
4. Rate specific phenomena independently.
5. Well acquaint with the recording instrument.

The use of observation as a method of data collection, depends upon the researcher's prejudices and biases, his powers of perception, his outlook, his ability to recognise casual relationship or sequences and his accuracy in recording the results of his observation.

2. INTERVIEW

Interview is one of the chief means of collecting data in Social Science Research. Interview may be defined as a systematic conversation initiated for a specific purpose and focused on certain planned content areas. it is not a simple two-way conversation between an investigator and an informant.

The investigator is asking someone to respond to specific questions relating to his opinions or experiences or attitudes or values or beliefs or future intentions or knowledge. The interviewing is done with the help of a structured schedule or an interview guide. It may be used as a main method or a supplementary one.

In an empirical study (field oriented study) the interview plays a major role. The Linds in their study of Middle town interviewed all classes and ranks of society. Kinsey and associates interviewed thousands of people, including children regarding sex habits and practices.[1]

2.1 ADVANTAGES OF INTERVIEW AS A RESEARCH TOOL

All types of persons whether educated or uneducated can be covered by this method. Interview is a highly flexible tool. If respondent is not able to understand a question, he can get clarification from the interviewer. For assessing personal qualities of an interviewee such as emotions, opinions and reactions, the interviewer has to make observations at the time of interview. The subtle feelings and emotions of the respondents can be known through the interview.

It is generally assumed that the personal interview helps to obtain the most accurate information. The presence of the interviewer has some effect on the accuracy of data obtained. It is hard for the respondents to report incorrectly. Interviewers can probe and secure explanation.

Interviewing is a process of social interaction. A good poker player wins the play not only due to his knowledge of the cards but also due to his skill in guessing about his opponents. In the same way the interviewer must not only be conscious of the real meaning of the answers given by the interviewee, but he must also be aware that the respondent is guessing at the initiation of the interviewer. The respondent will give more information because he feels that the interviewer already knows much.

2.2 TYPES OF INTERVIEWS

Interviews generally fall into three broad categories: authoritative, historical and field oriented.

Authoritative interview is meant for gathering information from an authority. The researcher may interview a banking authority regarding the exact procedures for extending loans to business.

Historical interview is meant to gather information about a specific event from an individual who was present at the time or someone who knew it. An interview with a freedom fighter is an historical interview.

The field interview is conducted to learn how people feel about themselves and others, about their environment, and about specific issues and problems. An interview with bank employees, to study their job satisfaction is a field interview.

On the basis of the mode of conducting interview, it is classified into five types — structured interview, non-structured interview, focused interview, depth interview and panel interview. In structured interview, a detailed schedule is used. A list of predetermined questions is used and it takes the form of a questionnaire. It is highly useful for administrative and market research of various types.

The non-structured interviews are free flowing interviews. A list of predetermined questions is not used. The researcher uses an interview guide. He encourages the interviewee to have free expression by such comments as 'Is it so?', 'Go ahead', etc.

Focused interview is focused on the reactions, attitude and emotional responses of persons in a particular situation under study such as a film seen by him and a radio programme listened to by him.

The depth interview aims at eliciting deeper feelings, emotions or convictions. It calls for specialised training on the part of the researcher, e.g., a survey on the attitudes to homosexuality. Some people feel strongly about it, some are too inhibited to talk about it and others are too glad to talk about it. A well-framed interview schedule will not be useful to understand the attitude of the respondents. If an interview is skilfully conducted the interviewer will be able to cut through any embarrassment and emotional inhibitions and dig as deep as possible to bring out the person's attitude. "When skilfully and cautiously used by an interviewer having specialised training, the depth interview can reveal important aspects of psycho-social situations which are otherwise not readily available and yet may be crucial for understanding observed behaviour and reported opinions and attitudes."[2]

The panel interview aims at the investigator calling on a respondent periodically and collecting the data for the periods between the two consecutive visits.

2.3 TECHNIQUES OF INTERVIEWS

The following guidelines will help the investigator in conducting meaningful and worthwhile interviews.

2.3.1 SET UP INTERVIEW TIME

Whenever possible the researcher should arrange for the interview in advance. when an interview is arranged in advance, the investigator should be punctual.

2.3.2 INTRODUCTION LETTER

The researcher should take with him an introduction letter from his institution. While interviewing respondents from rural or tribal areas, the researcher should secure the co-operation of their local leaders.

2.3.3 ESTABLISH RAPPORT WITH THE RESPONDENTS

The researcher should win the confidence of the respondents by disclosing his identity and explaining the purpose of the interview in the way in which the respondent can understand. He should remove barriers to initial communication. Some respondents may suspect that the interviewer is a government agent and the information may be used against him. Such suspicion should be cleared before undertaking the interview.

2.3.4 ALLAY THE FEAR OF THE RESPONDENTS

Some respondents may be diffident of answering questions. Such kind of anxiety has to be allayed by using the following statements. This is just a survey. There is no right or wrong answer. I am simply trying to learn from your experience.

2.3.5 INTERVIEW ATMOSPHERE

The atmosphere should be friendly. The interview should be carried on in an informal, natural and conversational style. The whole interview should be conducted in an easy, natural and relaxed manner.

2.3.6 TECHNICAL DEVICES

Electronic equipments have advanced the art of interview and the researcher can make a good use of these devices. The researcher has the advantage of obtaining the exact record of the questions and answers.

2.3.7 BE ON THE BRASS-TRACKS

Diversion from the main subject may be interesting and valuable. But the researcher should tactfully bring the interviewee back to the brass-tracks and continue the interview.

2.3.8 PRESENCE OF OTHER PEOPLE

At the time of interview no one except the interviewer and the interviewee should be present.

2.3.9 OFF-THE-RECORD REMARKS

The researcher should consider the request of the interviewee that certain information should be off the record. The investigator should get him back on the records as tactfully and as quickly as possible.

2.3.10 QUESTIONS

The questions asked in the interview should be clear, concise and pertinent. Ask one question at a time. If a question is not understood, it should be repeated. The interviewer should not reveal his own opinions. Even when he is asked for his views, he can laugh off the request with some remarks as 'well, I have not thought about' or 'your opinions are more important than mine.'

2.3.11 CONTROVERSIAL MATTERS

In some interviews, the interviewer is confronted with the problem of opinions and values. The interviewer is not a debator and he should neither argue nor dispute. He should not try to educate or impose his own opinions on him. He should maintain an impartial and objective attitude.

2.3.12 LESS TALK

The interviewer draws information from another person, without informing him of his views and ideas. The major portion of the talk should be of the interviewee and not of the interviewer.

2.3.13 ATTAIN A PROPER EXIT

Leave the interviewee with the feeling that he has really contributed something. Such frame of mind of the interviewer will enable him to approach the interviewee in future for any study and interviewees will also participate willingly.

2.4 LIMITATIONS OF THE INTERVIEW

Inspite of many advantages cited already, interview as a method of collection of primary data has many limitations.

The interview is influenced by the emotional set up of the interviewee. the hesitancy to report facts and his urge to please or antogonise the interviewer will affect the interview. Interviewer and interviewee live in two different worlds of discourse. They have different social philosophies and ascribe different values and meanings to social phenomena. Their points of view and interests may clash. Hence any move to please the interviewee will also affect the study.

The stresses and strains of either the interviewer or interviewee or both will influence the interview. Poor memory of and inability to articulate on the part of the interviewee affect the interview. The omissions and mistakes in recording of the interview by the investigator affect the interview. The differences in the perception and understanding of the interviewer and interviewee also affect the accuracy of the data.

Interviewers often approach their respondents with a prepared set of expectations. This bias may distort and invalidate the results of the whole interview. The structured interview imposes selection of topics and controls the content of responses and undermines the accuracy of the data.

The potential interviewees cannot be contacted because they are not found in their houses. Sometimes they cannot be contacted since they are busy during office hours. It is also a common phenomenon that many potential interviewees randomly selected are bound to be unsuitable for an interview.

The percentage of selected interviewees who refuse to participate in personal interview will vary from project to project. The interviewee is not willing to answer certain questions because he is of highly personal nature.

2.5 INTERVIEW GUIDE

Interview guide is a written document giving an outline of the different aspects to be studied. It gives a general plan for the interview, various topics that are to be discussed, and some important questions. Interview guide gives direction for an interview.

3. TELEPHONE INTERVIEW

The data collection technique through survey is classified into three categories such as mail, personal interview and telephone interview. The selection of the most appropriate technique is not difficult. Three elements must be considered. First and foremost is the match between research requirements and the attributes of the alternate techniques. Secondly, the availability of funds and the coverage of the survey come into play. Finally, the immediacy of the responses is essential. The telephone interview is an economic method of collecting data in a short period.

There are two primary tasks in organising a telephone survey. One is to design the survey instrument itself. The other is to select a set of respondents.

3.1 TELEPHONE INTERVIEW SCHEDULE

The language of the telephone interview schedule may be a little different from in-person interview schedule. It may require a few more verbal clarification statements such as "Ok"? "Do you understand"? Is that clear"? or "Can we continue"? These are necessary because the interviewer cannot see the respondent's reactions.

Open-ended questions are to be answered more perfunctorily on the telephone. If the interviewer wants multiple answers to a question, it will be difficult to get more than two responses on the telephone.

3.2 SELECTING A SAMPLE

There are numerous ways of selecting a set of telephone numbers to represent the population to be sampled. The method chosen will depend on the size of the area as well as the size of the survey.

In the early days of telephone interview, telephone directories were used. In rural and non-metropolitan areas, most households are listed in the directory. In large cities directories may exclude more than one-third of the residential telephone numbers. To get around this problem first numbers are selected from the directory, then the last three digits in each are replaced with random numbers. In this way, unlisted numbers will have a chance of being selected. Most localities also have cross-index telephone directories, which list phone numbers by address or by numerical ordering. Such directories are highly useful.

The newer way to select a telephone sample does not use telephone directories at all. Instead the use of random-digit dialing (RDD) obviates the need for the telephone book. RDD uses a computer to select the numbers to be called. If the sample is to represent some regional area of India or of the country as a whole the RDD is much useful. This can be done by stratifying the computer's choices, first on the basis of the area codes (the three-digit-numbers that must be used first to call long-distance) and, second, on the basis of the three-digit local exchange or prefixes which precede the last four suffixed numbers. In the USA there are about 100 area codes and 30000 exchanges. The area codes are given in most directories, and the exchanges may be selected from telephone directories or obtained from the telephone exchange.

3.3 MERITS OF TELEPHONE SURVEY

Interviewing respondents over the telephone has become popular in recent years. It is easier to call individuals on the telephone than to go out for interview. The advantages of telephone interviewing are three in number.

(1) Cost of telephone survey is low, (2) telephone survey needs less time and effort, and (3) telephone survey is more impersonal.

Low cost : Telephone Interview is less expensive. Groves and Kahn (1979) of the University of Michigan's Survey Research Centre found out the cost of telephone survey and in person survey. The different components of the cost are the following :

Sl. No.	*Cost Components*	*Telephone Survey (in percentage)*	*In Person Survey (in percentage)*
1.	Cost of selecting sample	2.50	10.00
2.	Training and pre-study work	5.40	11.20
3.	Cost of fixed staff	00.00	20.00
4.	Telephone charges	41.00	00.00
5.	Communication charges	0.00	7.00

Except telephone charges all other charges are the lowest in telephone survey.

3.3.1 TIME AND EFFORT

Telephone interview consumes less time, since it involves contact of people by phone than to go out and talk to them. It has been estimated that the total hours spent in the telephone survey of 1500 participants equalled 5419 hours as compared with 13,522 hours in the in-person survey. An average of 3.3 hours per interview for the telephone survey and 8.7 hours for in-person survey has been spent.

3.3.2 IMPERSONAL NATURE

In telephone interview, the respondent may be willing to divulge personal information than in a face-to-face encounter. There is less temptation to try to enhance one's image to a telephone interviewer.

3.4 DEMERITS OF TELEPHONE SURVEY

The disadvantages of telephone survey are the following :

Lack of Motivation : As there is no eye contact in the telephone interview, it is more difficult for the interviewer to assess the interest level of the respondent. The interviewer keeps the telephone conversation flowing so that the respondent does not have time to consider whether he or she is bored or too busy. Ultimately, the interviewer finds it difficult to obtain in-depth information from an open-ended question.

3.4.1 QUESTIONS WHICH DEPEND ON VISUAL CUES

In a telephone interview possible responses must be read out to the respondent for a selection. Where reactions to pictures or other visual cues are desired, the telephone is helpless. The advent of the video telephone would alter the receptivity of the respondents.

3.4.2 EASIER TO DENY

It is easier to deny to someone on that telephone than to deny to someone facing you. Hence, there is much scope for declining to answer the queries on phone.

3.4.3 GETTING WORKING HOUSEHOLD NUMBERS

For telephone surveys telephone numbers are usually selected from telephone directories. As telephone directories are not suitable, random digit dialing (RDD) is followed. The RDD produces many telephone numbers that are not of residential households. This creates what has been called the doss rate. Doss numbers are those which for one reason or other do not lead to households.

4. MAIL SURVEYS

The purpose of this essay is to describe the techniques used for professional mail surveys to enable the readers to acquaint with the procedures used in mail surveys.

There are three main types of surveys, depending on the method of data gathering used: personal interview surveys, telephone surveys and mail surveys. The basic distinction between the mail and other types of surveys is the fact that in surveying by mail, there is no person to ask questions and guide the respondent. This gives rise to important differences in survey design, questionnaire construction and various other aspects of the survey.

The first mail survey was conducted in 1577 by King Philip II of Spain. He conducted a census of his New World Possession. A questionnaire in the form of a memorandum and detailed instructions were sent to overseas governors and other top government officials. Since mail service was not known in those days the survey was conducted by courier. The percentage of return was very satisfactory since the filled up questionnaires furnished the information required by the king.

4.1 ADVANTAGES OF MAIL SURVEYS

There are ten major advantages of mail surveys. Let us analyse each of these advantages.

4.1.1 WIDER DISTRIBUTION

Personal interview surveys are clustered in a limited number of cities and an even more restricted number of rural areas since sending an interviewer to different areas is costly. But the mail man has no difficulty in reaching different areas. There is no special problem in reaching rural as well as urban homes or in surveying any number of different countries.

4.1.2 LESS DISTRIBUTION BIAS

The interviewers have aversion to visit the people living in their neighbourhood. In such areas specially trained interviewers of particular race or religion are needed. There is also the difficulty of reaching some families since it will be harder to make an appointment with the people holding high positions. Moreover, it is hard to reach all members of a family since the interviewer cannot reach them.

The mail is delivered to the addressee's home and will be there whenever he arrives. Whenever an individual is in a hospital, on a business trip or on vacation, the mail will reach him sooner or later.

4.1.3 NO INTERVIEWER BIAS

Even the appearance, clothing, tone of voice, urgency and manners of an interviewer may influence the answers. The appearance of the interviewer — beautiful or ugly, fair or black, elegant or seedy, young or old — may subtly bias the mind of the respondent.

The anonymity of the respondent and the fact that his answers will be confidential can be made very clear in the letter accompanying a mail questionnaire. This will produce more reliable answers.

4.1.4 THOUGHTFUL REPLY

The respondent getting the questionnaire by mail has a chance to think over and he can fill it up at his leisure. But in a telephone interview, when the phone rings and the interviewer asks certain questions, the respondent has only few minutes to answer the questions.

4.1.5 CENTRALISED CONTROL

Mail surveys can be done from one office with built-in checks and controls for every phase of the operation. On a major personal interview, hundreds of interviews have to be instructed, supervised and checked, with special controls by region, state or city. In the mail survey it is easier to keep up the quality of data gathering by means of the centralised control.

4.1.6 COST-SAVING

The services of mailmen cost less than those of interviewers of the same country. In the case of interview the interviewers have to be given training which is costly. Besides this, there are also briefing, supervision and checking. Moreover, remuneration must be paid to the investigators.

4.2 LIMITATIONS

In some cases the mail survey method is inappropriate and at other times its uses are limited. Some of the limitations of the mail survey are given below:

4.2.1 PROBLEM OF THE MAILING LIST

There is no readily available mailing list and the construction of a mailing list would be expensive. The available list is incomplete and such incompleteness will make it impossible to conduct a reliable mail survey.

4.2.2 QUESTIONNAIRE PROBLEM

In the case of depth interviews, where the information required from the respondents can not be structured, it is often impossible to construct a questionnaire.

If a questionnaire runs to more than six and eight pages the response to a mailing falls sharply. It may not be possible to conduct a mail survey if the questions and answers are more time-consuming or require too much concentration or checking of documents or consulting of other people. Sometimes the information required is confidential. If a company has a strict rule that its sales or purchasing figures are to be kept confidential no survey will succeed in getting at them.

4.2.3 THE RESPONDENT IS NOT FILLING UP THE QUESTIONNAIRE

It may happen that a wife fills up the questionnaire addressed to her husband or an assistant or secretary completes a form for the boss. This problem exists in questionnaires sent to home address.

4.3 TYPES OF MAIL SURVEYS

The following are few kinds of surveys used by business and industry and they are conducted by mail. Similar techniques are often used in surveys conducted by the government or in the field of science.

4.3.1 INDUSTRIAL AND CONSUMER SURVEYS

Industrial Surveys are studies conducted among manufacturers, wholesalers or dealers by suppliers of manufactured products designed for industrial use. These surveys seek answers to such questions as How useful is the product? How does it compare with other brands of the same product? In what ways is it better? Does it fail to measure up to its competitors in any of its qualities? How large is the market for this product? Is it expanding or contracting? What are its prospects in the future? etc..

This type of research can be done by mail because most industrial suppliers and manufacturers have a list of customers and prospective customers which can be sampled for industrial mail surveys.

4.3.2 MEDIA STUDIES

Advertisers, their agencies and the media themselves want to know who is reached by the medium, who reads the message and what relationship is there between the medium and the people it reaches. Publications often survey their subscribers and readers to find out their demographic characteristics, what they own or plan to buy, in what leisure time activities they engage, their investments, the influence they wield in their businesses and their communities. Business, government, professional and student groups are surveyed by mail to find out what they read, and what they watch on TV and how often and what they listen to on the radio and for how long.

4.3.3 SURVEYS ON ADVERTISING

Advertising copy or complete advertisements can be tested either by sending versions of the advertisement with a questionnaire or by sending a questionnaire to the people in a controlled area.

Another form of advertising research is the readership traffic study. Newspapers mail out a copy of representative issue to random sample of subscribers one day after the subscriber has received his regular copy of the same issue. The accompanying letter asks him to use the enclosed red pencil to mark every advertisement which he has seen in that particular issue and to return it. The resulting analysis will furnish valuable data on the effect of subject matter, size, position, presence or absence of illustration and other variables upon the effectiveness of advertising appearing in the same paper.

Finally, in some cases advertising penetration and the effects of advertising can be checked by mail surveys. Such surveys aim at determining the percentage of people who remembered various slogans or the percentage who were induced by some advertisements to buy a product or visit a show room.

4.3.4 MULTIPLE SURVEYS AND PANELS

The survey can be conducted among several groups of people for example users of a product, potential users and other non-users. The findings can frequently furnish a deeper and more meaningful analysis.

The members of a panel agree in advance that they will answer questionnaires; the researcher has to establish the sample only once. The percentage of response will always be high and the questionnaires will be well answered.

4.4 SURVEY DESIGN

The good researcher will carefully plan every step of a survey before actually taking one. The following steps are the logical and essential parts of survey design :

(i) Outlining the problem.
(ii) Definition of research objectives.
(iii) Investigating existing research on the same problem.
(iv) Definition of the Universe.
(v) Deciding on the degree of reliability aimed at within a realistic budget.
(vi) Definition of the sample and scope.
(vii) Deciding on the survey method.
(viii) Deciding who will conduct survey.
(ix) Establishing the techniques.
(x) Tabulation, analysis and report.
(xi) Timing.
(xii) Cost estimate.

4.5 MAILING LIST

If the survey is a census, the mailing list will contain the name and address of every member of the universe. If the research problem concerns a large universe, it is not necessary to survey every member of the population. Whether the study is based on census method or sampling method, a mailing list is needed. The mailing list should be free from bias.

4.6 SAMPLING

A sample is a part of the population. The sample should be representative of the population and the information obtained must be reliable. In any survey where reliability is desired, the errors and variances have to be controlled, measured and interpreted. it is a job for trained statisticians to plan and supervise sample design and sampling operations. The researcher conducting the mail survey must get the help of the statisticians.

4.7 QUESTIONNAIRE CONSTRUCTION

The questionnaire is the tool used to collect data from the respondent. A good questionnaire appears as easy to compose as does a good poem. The subjects to be included should have been selected at the time the survey design was established. The questionnaire should take into consideration the completeness and relevance of data, the short and easy look, paper and printing, lay-out, check versus open-end questions and the like. For details see the chapter on Questionnaire Construction.

4.8 COST ESTIMATING AND SCHEDULING

There are three considerations which are important in estimating survey costs :

(i) All items which add to cost should be included.

(ii) The cost of each item should be ascertained carefully.

(iii) Timing, in so far as it affects cost should be carefully considered.

In order to establish a realistic target date for completing a mail survey a schedule must be established. This will enable the researcher to plan and control the flow of work and its timing. The following are some of the points to be taken into account in constructing a schedule.

(i) Sufficient time should be allotted for each operation.

(ii) The schedules should translate the number of hours needed for each operation.

(iii) The schedule should specify starting and completion dates for the various operations.

(iv) The schedule should function as an automatic control over the flow of work.

4.9 PILOT STUDIES

It is obvious that pilot studies can guide the researcher and improve the quality of the mail survey. The pilot studies enable the researcher to test the quality of the mailing list and check the percentage of return, the effectiveness, the occurrence of bias and the usefulness of information and the establishment of cost estimate.

4.10 ADVANCE NOTICE OF THE QUESTIONNAIRE

Many tests have shown that the percentage of return can be increased by an advance notice. The simplest and least expensive way of announcing a survey is to send out advance post cards. It should be timed to reach two to five days before the questionnaire is despatched. The easiest form to use is the standard government post card. The copy will depend upon the nature of survey, but it has to be short, polite and to the point. The effect of the post card can be increased by referring to it on the outgoing envelope which contains the questionnaire.

An advance letter serves approximately the same purpose as the post card and generally the same rules apply to it. Telephone introduction of a mail questionnaire is a rather expensive method for giving advance information. This is effective when the research project involving a lengthy questionnaire requiring special effort.

4.11 THE ACCOMPANYING LETTER

The accompanying letter represents an important step in the effort to get a high percentage of the questionnaires mailed. It induces the reader to complete and return the enclosed questionnaire.

4.12 MAILING PROCEDURE

Before assembling the mailing piece and actually putting all the elements in the outer envelope, the researcher has to make sure that they have all been processed properly and are ready for final operation. The nature and sequence of mailing operations may vary according to the size of the mailing and the degree of automation used. The possible plan for mailing is given below :

(i) Prepare instructions for printing, keying and mailing.
(ii) Print Questionnaires.
(iii) Key Questionnaires.
(iv) Type or process list cards.
(v) Key list cards (numbering).
(vi) Processing accompanying letters.
(vii) Address envelopes.
(viii) Personalise letters and place each letter under the flap of its envelope.
(ix) Process the address into the reply envelope.
(x) Stamp the reply envelope.
(xi) Place the incentive coin.
(xii) Fold the letter and stuff the envelope.
(xiii) Check by the Supervisor (Researcher).
(xiv) Seal and Stamp.
(xv) It is advisable to get a receipt from the post office.

4.13 FOLLOW-UP MAILINGS

The primary purpose of follow-up mailings is to reduce the percentage of non-respondents and thereby make the survey more representative. A high percentage of response is achieved by the first mailing and the follow-up mailing will always produce some more returns. Every sample consists of three types of individuals.

(i) Eager beavers, who love to answer practically anything.
(ii) Just people, who are more or less uninterested in answering questions, but who can be induced to do so.
(iii) Born non-respondents.

The follow-up mailings are aimed at group two. On receipt of the filled up questionnaires from the eager beavers, number them and send a follow-up mailing only to non-respondents.

A remainder post card is usually sent out three to five days after the first mailing and is mailed to the entire sample. This is a reminder and not a "follow-up" or "second wave." The second wave will contain another copy of the questionnaire and a reply envelope identical with those used in the first mailing. The accompanying letter will be different. The second wave can be mailed to non-respondents when the returns from the wave start petering out. The third and successive waves may be sent out by mail or by wire or they may consist of telephone or personal intimation.

4.14 THE NON-RESPONSE PROBLEM

It is impossible to achieve a 100 per cent response. Favourable circumstances combined with careful planning and repeated efforts result in unusually high rates of response. There are several reasons such as mislaid, overlooked answering, already filled out and returned questionnaire, too busy at the time, away from house, non-receipt of the questionnaire, not interested in the subject of research and reluctant to answer questionnaires.

REFERENCES

1. Pauline V. Young, *Scientific Social Surveys and Research*, (New Delhi : Prentice Hall of India Private Limited, 1984), p. 217.
2. Pauline V. Young, *Scientific Social Surveys and Research*, (New Delhi : Prentice Hall of India Private Limited, 1984), p. 220.

CHAPTER FIVE

SECONDARY DATA

1. SIGNIFICANCE OF SECONDARY DATA

The sources of information that a researcher should tap vary with his interest and the type of study he has undertaken. The sources of information are classified into field and documentary sources.

The data from field sources may be collected from persons who have amassed a fund of knowledge about social conditions through observation, interview, questionnaire and other devices. Primary data are generally used in those cases where the secondary data do not provide an adequate basis for analysis.

A considerable amount of data are available in the published and unpublished documents, reports, manuscripts, letters, diaries and so on. Data obtained from published and unpublished records of governmental or public bodies are called secondary data. The reason why secondary data are being increasingly used is that published statistics are now available from various agencies.

The secondary data may be collected from primary sources, secondary sources and tertiary sources of information. The primary sources of information include first hand accounts of experimentation and investigation (articles in professional journals, doctoral theses, monographs and questionnaires), original works (letters, diaries, poems, novels, autobiographies) and reports testimony, report of government departments and agencies, annual reports and minutes).

Secondary sources of information are summaries of information gathered from primary sources. These include translations, summaries, and reviews of research (encyclopaedia, articles) abstracts, guide books and other publications containing factual information, commentaries and so on.

Tertiary sources of information include text books. Text books are generally compiled from secondary sources of information and some text books have become the authoritative sources of information.

1.1 SIGNIFICANCE OF SECONDARY DATA

The primary data collected by one person may become the secondary data to another. The census survey conducted by the Government of India once in 10 years collects primary data about the people of the country. But the same statistics will become secondary data to anyone else There are certain distinct advantages of and limitations to using secondary data.

1.1.1 ADVANTAGES OF SECONDARY DATA

The various advantages of using secondary data are the following :

(i) It is highly economical, as less expenditure is incurred in the collection of secondary data. But in the case of collection of primary data enormous amount has to be spent at various stages of data collection starting from designing the tool of data collection upto the stage of tabulation of the data.

(ii) The secondary data facilitate the researcher to complete the research project promptly, since he need not spend much of his time in collecting data. When a research project is based on primary data enormous time has to be spent in designing the tool of data collection, collecting the data from the field and processing the collected data.

(iii) The secondary data help the researcher to formulate the research problem. The secondary data enable the researcher as well to prepare the tool of data collection and formulate hypotheses for the study.

(iv) The researcher could find research gap in the area of study with the help of the secondary data. The review of literature helps him to select the problem for an investigation.

(v) Finally secondary data can be used as a basis for comparison with the primary data that the researcher has just collected.

1.1.2 LIMITATIONS OF SECONDARY DATA

In practice one finds that secondary data do not fit perfectly into the framework of the research project under consideration. The numerous limitations prevalent in them form the reason for this.

(i) It is very difficult to assess the accuracy of the secondary data. It is also difficult to know with what care secondary data have been collected and tabulated.

(ii) A severe limitation in the use of secondary data is that they may be somewhat out of date. A good deal of time is spent in the collection, processing, tabulation and publishing of these data. By the time the data are made available to the researcher they may have become out dated due to excessive time consumed in their collection.

(iii) Finally the secondary data are not available to the researcher in the form he wants to have. For example the age of the households may be *(i)* Below 18, *(ii)* 18-28, *(iii)* 28-38, *(iv)* 38-48, *(v)* Above 58. If the researcher wants to group the households into *(i)* Below 20 *(ii)* 20-30 and so on, it cannot be done with the help of the secondary data.

2. EVALUATION SECONDARY DATA

Robert W. Joselyn suggests a detailed approach for evaluating secondary data and understanding the potential limitations. The approach comprises eight steps. These eight steps are grouped into three categories namely: *(i)* Project objectives; *(ii)* Cost of acquisition; and *(iii)* Accuracy of data. The eight steps are found in the answers to the eight questions, which are listed below :

(i) Do the data help to answer questions set out in the problem definitions?

(ii) Do the data apply to the population of interest?

(iii) Do the data apply to the time period of interest?

(iv) Can the units and classifications presented, be applied?

(v) Is it possible to get at the original sources of the data?

(vi) Is the cost of data acquisition worthy of it?

(vii) Is there the possibility of bias?

(viii) Can the accuracy of data collection be verified?

The answers to these questions will no doubt help the researcher to evaluate the utility of the secondary data which can be used for the study.

3. SOURCES OF SECONDARY DATA

The main sources of secondary data are the following :

3.1 BIBLIOGRAPHIES

A bibliography mostly contains particulars of books and articles published in a particular discipline. It is highly useful for verifying a reference to a publication, which has been quoted incomplete or inaccurate in some other sources. The following are the important bibliographies useful to Social Science Research.

3.1.1 THE UNITED STATES CATALOGUE

It is an author, subject, and title index to publications issued in the United States of America since 1898. Since 1928 this catalogue has included publications issued in English in Canada and other English speaking countries.

3.1.2 INTERNATIONAL BIBLIOGRAPHY OF SOCIAL SCIENCES

This bibliography is published by UNESCO annually in four parts — Sociology, Political Science, Economics and Anthropology. This bibliography is published in English and French and includes both author and subject indexes.

3.1.3 INDIAN NATIONAL BIBLIOGRAPHY

It is an authoritative record of current publications in the 15 major languages of India. All those received by the National Library, Calcutta are included in this bibliography.

3.1.4 INDIANA

A selected list of references and representative books on all aspects of Indian life and culture edited by Shri B. Sengupta, and published by World Press, Calcutta in 1966.

3.1.5 THE LIBRARY OF CONGRESS ACCESSION LIST, SOUTH ASIA

This is a monthly record of all publications brought out in Afghanistan, Bangladesh, Bhutan, India, Maladives, Nepal, Pakistan and Sri Lanka. The literature survey in this document mainly includes political, economic and social developments and international relations of the countries of Asia.

3.2 INDICES

Indexes concentrate more on periodical literature. A list of articles is called an index. The important sources for locating periodical articles are indicated below.

3.2.1 SOCIAL SCIENCE INDEX

This index is published by H.W. Wilson Co., New York and appears in two parts namely, Social Sciences Index and Humanities Index.

3.2.2 INDEX INDIA

This index is being published by the Rajasthan University from 1967. This is a quarterly documentation consisting of Indian Newspaper Index, Index to Indian Periodicals, Index to Foreign Periodicals, Index to Composite Publications, Index to Biographical Profiles, Index to Book Reviews and Index to theses and documents.

3.2.3 THOMPSON INDICES

Hindustan Thompson Associates brings out a compendium of data on urban and rural India. This is compiled in two separate editions :

(i) Thompson Urban Market Index; and

(ii) Thompson Rural Market Index.

The Urban Market Index is divided into two parts. The first part consists of market indices of various cities and urban agglomerations. The second part consists of information on 46 demographic and socio-economic variables for each city.

The Rural Market Index takes the district as the basic unit. The data are presented against 23 indicators and the Index covers 383 districts.

3.2.4 GUIDE TO INDIAN PERIODICAL LITERATURE

It is a quarterly, published by Indian Documentation Science, Gurgaon. It contains author and subject index to articles, research papers, notes, conference proceedings and book reviews from about 300 Indian journals in social sciences and humanities. It is a basic research tool on social sciences in India.

3.3 ABSTRACTS

Abstracts give a gist of the content of an article, book, dissertation and the like. The details given in an index are author, title, periodicity, publisher and a brief summary of the important points of the periodical article that is being indexed. The important abstracts are the following.

3.3.1 INDIAN DISSERTATION ABSTRACTS

ICSSR publishes synopsis of Ph.D. theses in the Social Sciences submitted to Indian Universities. Each synopsis gives the name of the University awarding the degree, the year and name of the supervisor. In March 1973 Volume No.1 was brought out. The disciplines included within the scope of this abstract are Economics, Education, Management, Public Administration, Sociology, Social Science aspect of Anthropology, Demography, Geography, History, Law and Linguistics.

3.3.2 INDIAN BEHAVIOURAL SCIENCE ABSTRACTS

This document is published quarterly by Behavioural Science Centre, 32 Subash Marg. Delhi. It contains abstracts of behavioural science literature produced in Indian or abroad. It covers fields such as Psychology, Sociology, Social Anthropology, Economics, Education, Management, Political Science, Public Administration, Extension Education, Social Work, History and Human Geography. It provides abstracts of articles, books and research publications as well as unpublished doctoral, master's and diploma theses.

3.3.3 ABSTRACTS AND INDEX OF REPORTS AND ARTICLES

The Lok Sabha Secretariat publishes a digest of significant books, articles, Parliament reports and the like.

3.3.4 UNIVERSITY NEWS

The Association of Indian Universities publish the University News which has a column to indicate the particulars of doctoral dissertations accepted by Indian Universities.

3.4 STATISTICAL SOURCES

A large variety of data on social problems are regularly published by governments and other agencies in most of the countries of the world. The most frequently consulted statistical publications are the following :

1. United Nations Statistical Year Book, published annually by the UN Department of Economic and Social Affairs, New York.
2. Demographic Year Book published by the UN Department of Economic and Social Affairs, New York containing statistics from every country of the world.
3. Production Year Book published by Food and Agriculture Organisation, Rome contains data on all aspects of food and agriculture.
4. Census publications in India is the largest single source of data in respect of land and its people.
5. Statistical Abstracts is an annual publication brought out by Central Statistical Organisation, Government of India, providing data on different sections of the economy.
6. The Annual publication of the Union Ministry of Agriculture and Irrigation contains data regarding Indian agriculture.
7. Labour Statistics published annually by the Ministry of Labour, Government of India gives data regarding labour.

The periodical data many government and non-governmental agencies bring out are indicated below. The Market Research and Statistical Bureau of the Coffee Board, Bangalore publishes coffee statistics annually. The Coir Board, Cochin brings out annually its publications entitled "India's Production, Exports and Internal Consumption of Coir and Coir Goods." The Rubber Board Kottayam (Kerala) publishes the Indian Rubber Statistics annually. The Indian Sugar Mills Association, Delhi issues annually the Indian Sugar Year Book containing detailed statistics. The Steel Authority of India Limited (SAIL) publishes on a quarterly basis, statistics for the iron and steel industry in India. The Indian Woollen Mills Federation, Bombay brings out the quarterly publication "Wool and Woollens in India."

3.5 DIRECTORIES

Directories provide current information on subjects of common interest. The important directories are the following.

3.5.1 DIRECTORY OF SOCIAL SCIENCE RESEARCH INSTITUTIONS IN INDIA

This directory has been compiled by the Indian Council of Social Science Research, New Delhi. The directory covers research institutions in the field of Social Sciences, which are outside the university system.

3.5.2 BOMBAY STOCK EXCHANGE DIRECTORY

It contains information on financial accounts and key profitability and other ratios of listed joint stock companies. The directory has been designed in such a manner that the latest possible write-up on the listed companies can be inserted and the old one taken out.

3.5.3 DIRECTORY OF LIBRARIES

Indian Library Association brought out in 1951 the third edition of Indian Library Directory and the directory is being updated. The Indian Association of Special Libraries and Information Centres brought out a directory in 1962, which is being updated from time to time. The Government of India Librarian Association has released the Directory of Government of India Libraries and Who's Who in 1983.

3.6 YEAR BOOKS

Year books contain current information collected from a variety of sources. The important year books available to researchers are the following.

3.6.1 THE AMERICAN YEAR BOOK

It has been published since 1911. It is an excellent review of events of the year. The material is presented in articles grouped under broad subjects.

1. Statesman's Year Book (London : Macmillan and Company Limited), gives political, economic and social data for the countries of the world.
2. Municipal Year Book (Chicago: International City, Manager's Association) gives a detailed review of economic, political and social statistics relating to municipal governments.
3. Year book published by the Union of International Association, Brussells contains information regarding international organisations.
4. The annual, 'India' published by the Ministry of Information and Broadcasting, Government of India gives data regarding the development programmes undertaken by the government.
5. Kothari's Economic and Industrial Guide of India published by Kothari & Sons, Madras annually gives an analytical study of Annual Reports and Financial Documents of Indian Companies.

3.7 ENCYCLOPEDIAS

Encyclopedias contain informational articles on subjects in every field of knowledge usually arranged in alphabetical order. The two important encyclopedias are International Encyclopedias of the Social Sciences edited by David L. Sills, New York Macmillan & Co. and Free Press and Encyclopedia of the Social Sciences edited by Edwin R.A. Sobigman, New York Macmillan & Co., 16 volumes.

3.8 PERSONAL DOCUMENTS

Personal documents include autobiographies, letters, diaries, school essays, prize essays and the like. These documents will be highly useful in studying the life history of an individual or organisation.

Besides the sources of secondary data discussed above, other sources of secondary data are commemoration volumes, souvenirs, the statements of accounts published by companies, chairman's speeches, reports of commodity exchange and stock exchange and news items and editorials of leading newspapers.

CHAPTER SIX

TOOLS FOR COLLECTION OF DATA

1. *Tests*
2. *Cumulative Record Cards*
3. *Schedule*
4. *Questionnaire*
5. *Pre-testing the Questionnaire*
6. *Pilot Study*

1. TESTS

In the field of education, educational and psychological tests are used to measure the achievement of the students, their personality traits and the like. There are various kinds of test such as achievement tests, diagnostic tests, intelligence tests, aptitude tests, attitude tests and personality tests. A brief discussion on these tests is given below.

1.1 ACHIEVEMENT TEST

A standardised test of achievement of the students on any school/college subject is administered. If a teacher wants to test the achievement of the students in a specific area according to the need, the test called teacher made test is made use of.

1.2 DIAGNOSTIC TEST

This test is designed to ascertain a person's strength and weakness in one or more areas of the field in which he is tested. It tries to find out the nature of the difficulties which a student is experiencing.

1.3 INTELLIGENCE TEST

Psychologists and educationists have prepared a large number of intelligence tests for measuring the intelligence of children. Intelligence is measured in terms of intelligence quotient (IQ). The intelligence quotient represents the ratio of the mental age of the child to his chronological age. This ratio is multiplied by hundred for obtaining an integral value of quotient. The IQ gives an index of the ability.

1.4 APTITUDE TEXT

An aptitude is a person's conditions, a pattern of traits and demand to be indicative of his potentialities. Aptitude tests are useful for class room research and research in trade and industry.

1.5 ATTITUDE TEST

An attitude is a personality disposition or a drive which determines behaviour towards certain type of person, object, situation, institution or concept. An attitude is always directed towards something. Some persons have positive attitude towards untouchability. They like the idea of untouchability, believe in it, preach it and also act accordingly. Others have negative attitude towards untouchability. They hate the idea of untouchability and preach for the eradication of this evil from the society. In schools some children develop negative attitudes towards the institution or studies. They hate the institution and do not recognise its values.

1.6 PERSONALITY TEST

Personality is the most characteristic integration of an individual's structures, modes of behaviour, interests, aptitude capacities, abilities and attitude. Personality tests are designed to measure the personality traits of the individuals. Some of the personality traints are co-operation discipline, leadership, orderliness, personal appearance, punctuality, patriotism, responsibility, self confidence and team spirit.

1.7 CHARACTERISTICS OF A GOOD TEST

Before selecting a test for the research purposes, one should make sure that it possesses the following characteristics.

1.7.1 RELIABILITY

A reliable test is a trustworthy tool. A good test must measure accurately and consistently.

1.7.2 VALIDITY

It must actually measure what it is supposed to measure.

1.7.3 OBJECTIVITY

It must be objective. It is an important factor that affects both the validity and reliability of a test.

1.7.4 DISCRIMINATION

The test must detect and measure small differences in achievement, intelligence and the like. Each item of the test should discriminate between good and poor students if the test is used in educational research.

1.7.5 COMPREHENSIVENESS

A test should be comprehensive enough to be valid. It should include enough material so that it measures what it is supposed to measure.

1.7.6 USABILITY

Before using any test, the investigator should make sure whether he needs to collect the data related to the ability which that particular test measures.

2. CUMULATIVE RECORD CARDS

Cumulative record cards are very frequently used in educational research. If a researcher is interested in studying the achievements of a student in his hobbies, his personality traits, his practical and social activities, and his aptitudes, the cumulative record maintained in the school is referred to by the researcher. An adequate cumulative record provides the data essential to study the student's present situation in the light of his past development.

The cumulative cards are filled in and maintained by different class teachers. The investigator can obtain the required information ready-made by consulting the record cards of the students of a particular class under study.

In the field of commerce, researchers use cumulative record cards to study the market trends for agricultural commodities such as price, arrivals and sales.

3. SCHEDULE

Schedule is the most important tool. It is similar to a questionnaire. It is administered by the researcher in person and it is filled up by the researcher. As the schedule is presented in person it need not be attractive. The techniques of preparing questionnaire are also applied to framing an interview schedule. Hence the researchers are advised to refer to the questionnaire for more details.

4. QUESTIONNAIRE

Questionnaires are used primarily in making status studies of current practices and in conducting opinion polls and surveying attitudes. Questionnaire is a schedule to be filled up by an informant rather than by the researcher. The researcher must construct his questionnaire so cleverly as to elicit reliable and authentic information. The information is a competent source of data. The respondent must have the ability to understand the questions asked.

Questionnaire construction is an art. A good questionnaire is the product of long and painstaking work. The amateur researcher will often "construct" a four-page questionnaire in a few hours. For a professional research house this usually represents a week's work by several experienced people.

4.1 QUESTIONNAIRE DESIGN AND FORMAT

The researcher should decide what facts and opinion are to be sought for. He should also determine the persons to whom the questionnaire is to be sent.

The arrangement and appearance of the questionnaire is of prime importance is getting good returns. The format should be attractive. There should be minimum difficulty in passing from one question to another and filling in the intended responses.

Every questionnaire should contain either in its body or in a covering letter *(i)* a descriptive title for the study, *(ii)* purpose of the study, *(iii)* name of sponsoring agency or institution, *(iv)* name and address of the person to whom the completed questionnaire is to be returned, *(v)* the method of filling it up, and *(vi)* a guarantee that the identity of the respondent will not be revealed.

4.2 TYPES OF QUESTIONNAIRE

There are two types of questions. They are supply type and selection type.

The supply type of questions or open-ended questions allow the respondent to write what he feels about a topic. Such questions require a high standard of literacy. These questions demand a still greater amount of energy, willingness and care on the part of the respondent. As a consequence, unless the sample is carefully chosen and restricted to a literate group, the answers to such free questions are likely to be incomplete.

The selection type of questions may be Yes-No, True-False or Right-Wrong or multiple choice. This type of questions consists of statements to be answered categorically as Yes, or No, right, or wrong, true or false. These questions are dichotomous and they are convenient or least bothersome to respondents. In the case of multiple choice questions, the respondent is offered two or more choices. The respondent is likely to take more time to answer a multiple choice question.

4.3 CONSTRUCTION OF QUESTIONNAIRE

The following rules should be followed in the construction of questionnaire.[1]

(i) Express the items as clearly as possible.

(ii) Choose words that have precise meanings wherever possible.

(iii) Avoid complex or awkward word arrangement.

(iv) Include all qualifications needed to provide a reasonable basis for response selection.

(v) Avoid unessential specificity in the question or in the responses.

(vi) Avoid the inclusion of non-functional words in the item.

(vii) Avoid the inclusion of trivial questions.

(viii) Make the suggested answers as simple as possible.

(ix) Be sure that items will seem to the respondent to apply to the situation.

(x) Refrain from asking questions of opinion, unless opinion is specifically required.

(xi) Avoid items that are too suggestive or too unstimulating. They should not lead a respondent to go beyond the facts, but they should induce him to provide the required information.

(xii) Phrase questions to avoid the academically or socially acceptable responses. Make it possible for the respondent to answer truthfully without embarrassment.

(xiii) Avoid questions that may be checked with multiple responses when only one response is desired. In fact such items are usually quite difficult to tabulate and analyse.

(xiv) Whenever possible, questions should be worded in such a way that they can be answered simply by a check mark.

(xv) Ask questions in such a way that they will relieve the respondent of as much complex thinking as possible. A popular technique is to reduce a complex question to a series of questions which are easier to answer.

(xvi) Avoid the use of words which are susceptible to different interpretation, e.g., moral or immoral, good or bad, rich or poor, intelligent or ignorant, labourer or capitalist, etc.

4.4 PHYSICAL FORM OF THE QUESTIONNAIRE

The following features should be considered in the design of the questionnaire.

4.4.1 SIZE

The size of a questionnaire depends on the scope of the survey and the number of items to be included. Adequate space should be provided for recording the comments of the respondents. Only one space should be used for recording the responses. A normally designed questionnaire of monarch size (7 by 10 inches) can generally be expected to produce higher percentage of returns than one which is of letter head size (8 1/2 by 11 inches) and the letter head size will get a higher percentage of response than a legal sized sheet (8 1/2 by 14 inches).

4.4.2 NUMBER OF PAGES

The fewer the pages, the higher will be the percentage of return. By his experience the author would like to state that there is little justification for using the booklet form containing more pages. Normally, four (or maximum six) pages of a questionnaire, each page of the size of 8 1/2 by 11 inches, can be considered its optimum length.

4.4.3 LAY-OUT

The lay out should give the impression of a neat printed page which is easy to read and easy to fill up. The page should never be over crowded. If possible, the first page should be the shortest and easiest-looking page. It is advisable to group questions into sections by subject matter and start the numbering with question 1 for each section. Each section should have a heading that is descriptive and if possible, interesting.

4.4.4 INTERVIEWER INSTRUCTIONS

Directions for individual questions should be placed before or after the question depending on the nature of the direction. If the instructions deal with how the respondent should answer or how the question should be administered, then they should be placed before the question. If, on the other hand, the instructions relate to how the answers should be recorded or how the interview should probe, then they should be placed after the question. In order to distinguish instructions from questions, distinctive type (such as capitals or italics) is commonly used.

4.4.5 QUALITY AND COLOUR OF THE PAPER

The paper should be durable. White and light coloured questionnaires are preferable. When several questionnaires are sent in sequence, alternations of colours elicits more return than single colour. In these cases, light colours such as ivory, eye-case green, light yellow and light buff are recommended.

4.4.6 ARRANGEMENT OF ITEMS OF THE QUESTIONNAIRE

An attractive looking questionnaire enables the researcher to get the co-operation of the respondents. When the number of questions is large, they should be condensed in a very limited space.

4.4.7 COVERING LETTERS

The purpose of the questionnaire or study should be stated in the covering letter. Assurance should be given that the information wanted will be given confidential treatment. The request to participate in the study will stimulate responses from a large number of people.

4.4.8 FOLLOW-UP LETTERS

Follow-up letters are used in surveys where the questionnaires are placed and returned through the mail. In some surveys where the percentage of returns is small, the follow-up letters are very essential.

4.5 PRACTICAL PROBLEMS

It is difficult to make certain that the respondent has answered a question truthfully. There are many reasons :

(i) He may not know the answer.

(ii) He may not be thinking critically.

(iii) He may not have understood the directions correctly.

(iv) He may feel that the question is personal.

These difficulties can be minimised by the following steps :

(i) Creation of rapport through correspondence.

(ii) To allay suspicion on the part of the respondent; the purpose of the study must be made clear and he should be assured that his identity shall not be revealed.

(iii) Permission letter containing the signature of the project director, development head and administrative officer of the institution shall be attached to the questionnaire.

(iv) Use of return envelopes with stamps.

(v) Use of participate reply card.

(vi) Follow-up procedure.

(vii) Professional appearance of the questionnaire.

(viii) It is wise to formulate a preliminary draft and secure expert criticism on its make up and content. The draft should be submitted to a few individuals. In this way ambiguous questions, questions using unfamiliar words or words that are likely to cause confusion or misunderstanding can be brought to the researcher's attention.

5. PRE-TESTING THE QUESTIONNAIRE

Pretesting helps in enriching the design of the questionnaire and assists in testing the validity and reliability of statistical techniques to be adopted.

All aspects including layout, question sequence, word meaning, question difficulty, branching instructions and so on should be part of the pretest.

The pretest involves debriefing and/or protocol analysis. The procedure of asking the respondents to explain their answers, to state the meaning of each question and to describe any problems they had in answering or completing the questionnaire is called debriefing. The protocol analysis envisages thinking while completing the questionnaire.

The project director or person responsible for developing the questionnaire should conduct the pretest. The regular staff interviewers shall also conduct the pretest.

The respondents included in the pretest should be as similar as possible to the target population in terms of familiarity with the topic, general background characteristics and so on.

With a heterogenous target population a larger pretest sample will be required in order to conduct a critical pretest.

In the light of the pretest the questionnaire shall be modified.

6. PILOT STUDY

A pilot study is a small scale replica of the main study. The pilot study is a dress rehearsal and it provides guidance on the following :

(i) The adequacy of the sampling frame to be followed for the survey.

(ii) The pilot study enables the researcher to acquire prior knowledge about the population to be sampled.

(iii) The probable number of refusals and non-contacts can be roughly estimated from the pilot survey. As a result, a particular data collection method may be chosen in preference to others.

(iv) The suitable method of collecting the data from the alternative methods such as observation, questionnaire and interview schedule can be found out from the pilot study.

(v) The pilot study provides scope to make sure whether the wording in the questionnaire is simple, clear, unambiguous or free from technical terms.

(vi) The pilot study enables to test the efficiency of the instructions and general briefing of interviews. Sometimes the instructions may be adequate, but the interviewer may be doing a poor job.

(vii) The pilot study provides training to the interviewers.

(viii) The probable cost and duration of the main survey and its various stages will be known with the help of the pilot study. Pilot survey is valuable if the main survey is too long and too expensive.

6.1 CATEGORIES OF PILOT STUDIES

The categories of pilot studies are based on the purpose they serve:

(i) Testing the quality of the mailing list.

(ii) Checking the percentage of returns.

(iii) Checking the effectiveness of various segments of data-gathering process such as post cards, advance letters, incentives, and various types of follow-up efforts.

(iv) Checking the occurrence of bias resulting from the wording of cards, letters and questionnaires.

(v) Checking on how well questions are understood and answered.

(vi) Checking the usefulness of information received.

(vii) Checking or even establishing a cost estimate.

6.2 BASIC PRINCIPLES

Few basic principles which are to be borne in mind are given below :

(i) Each pilot study has to be conducted among a random sample of the universe surveyed. A biased sample as regards geographic division, sex, age or any other criterion would be wrong.

(ii) The number of questionnaire to be mailed in a test study should be large enough as to make the results meaningful for the purpose of the test.

(iii) We must not try to measure more than one variable at a time.

6.3 PILOT STUDIES ARE WORTH DOING

Pilot studies are sometimes omitted because of time and cost considerations. A little advance planning can reduce both the time and cost needed for testing. If the questionnaire is carefully constructed, the results of the test will not indicate the need for any major change.

It is obvious that pilot studies can guide the researcher and they considerably improve the quality of his research. Once the pilot study is over, the research worker should ask himself whether the study needs any modification either in the objectives of the study or in the scope of the study.

The size and design of the pilot study is a matter of convenience. The sample should be of comparable structure to that of main survey. The sample of the pilot study must be widespread as the main sample. If two forms of questions are to be compared, each question should be tried out. All the techniques of processing and analysis of data have to be piloted.

REFERENCE

1. Robert L. Ebel, "Writing the Test Item," in *Educational Measurement* (E.F. Lindquist, ed.), Washington, D.C., : American Council on Education, 1951, pp. 213-216.

CHAPTER SEVEN
HYPOTHESIS

1. INTRODUCTION

Once the researcher knows what his problem is, he can make a guess or number of guesses. The guesses he makes are the hypotheses which either solve the problem or guide him in further investigation. Hypothesis stands somewhat at the midpoint of research. From this midpoint one can go back to the problem and also look forward to the date. If the hypotheses is proved, the solution can be found. If it is not proved, alternative hypotheses need to be formulated and tested.

A great many social science investigations could not have been made without hypotheses. For example, psychologists have investigated the correlation between different kinds of abilities. Sociologists have studied the ecology of crime and of mental illness. Anthropologists have investigated the relationship between religious beliefs, marriage customs and other practices in a society.

2. SOURCES OF HYPOTHESIS

Hypotheses may be developed from various sources. Some of the important sources are the following :

(i) A hypothesis arises from intuition. These hypotheses have no clear connection with the large body of social science. The intuition is associated with an individual, who is influenced by environment.

(ii) A hypothesis also arises from other studies. The findings of a study may be formulated as hypotheses. The hypotheses followed in one study previously can be used in the present study.

(iii) Theory is a fertile seed-bed of hypotheses. For example, individuals who are rising in status are likely to be favourably inclined towards individual and objects that are helping their uplift in life. The researcher may identify the variables which influence the status of the said individuals.

(iv) Personal happiness provides scope for hypotheses. The phenomenon of personal happiness has been studied in great detail. Happiness has been correlated with income, education, occupation, social class and so on.

3. CHARACTERISTICS OF HYPOTHESES

Hypotheses should be empirically testable. It should be possible to draw certain inference, which in turn can be tested by observation in the field.

The hypotheses must be conceptually clear. The concepts utilised in the hypotheses should be clearly defined.

The hypotheses must be specific. Often the researchers are tempted to express their hypotheses in terms which are very general.

Hypotheses must be related to a study of theory or some theoretical orientation (e.g.) Minority community is greatly responsible for the growth of entrepreneurship in India.

4. ESTIMATION AND TESTING OF HYPOTHESIS

There are two objects of sample surveys. The first object is generally to estimate certain population parameters — the average of students in a college, the proportion of workers in a factory doing overtime work and so on. All sample results are subject to sampling errors.

The second purpose is to test a statistical hypothesis about a population. For example, the hypothesis that at least 80 per cent of the households in a town have TV sets. A sample of households is selected and the proportion of households possessing TV sets has been found out. It is evident that 77 per cent of the households have TV sets. The question now is whether the sample result is such as to discredit the hypothesis or whether it lends support to it. The deviation of the sample result from the hypothetical value can be judged.

There are two approaches to hypothesis testing — sampling theory approach and Bayesian approach.

The sampling theory approach is a traditional approach. It is found in all major statistics books. It is widely used in research. The decision making rests upon the sampling data. We establish a testing hypothesis which was rejected or accepted based on the sampling data.

The Bayesian approach is an extension of the classical approach, which uses sampling data for making decisions. It also incorporates all other information available to the decision makers. Most of the additional information consists of subjective probability estimates. The prior distribution may be revised after gathering information from the sample. The revised estimate known as a posterior distribution may be further revised by additional information and so on.

5. HYPOTHESIS TESTING PROCEDURE

The first step in testing the hypothesis is setting up of hypothesis. The conventional approach is to set up two hypothesis instead of one. If one hypothesis is true the other is false. Alternatively if one hypothesis is rejected then the other is accepted. These hypotheses are :

(i) Null hypothesis; and

(ii) Alternative hypothesis.

Following the sampling theory approach, we accept or reject a hypothesis on the basis of sampling information alone. Any sample we draw will vary from the population. We must judge whether these differences are statistically significant or insignificant.

Second step in choosing a statistical technique. There are many statistical tests, which are frequently used in hypothesis testing. They are z-test, t-test, F-test and x^2. The researcher should be able to choose the appropriate test. When the hypothesis pertains to a large sample (30 or more) the z-test is used. When the sample is less than 30, the t-test can be used. The choice of a test will depend upon a number of considerations such as number, variables involved, type of data, the size of the sample and whether the samples are independent or related.

The third step is the selection of desired level of significance. The confidence with which an experimenter rejects or retains a hypothesis depends upon the level of significance. The significance level is expressed in percentage such as 5%, 1% etc. When the researcher accepts 5% level, he will be making a wrong decision about 5% of the time. By rejecting the hypothesis at the same level, he runs the risk of rejecting a hypothesis in 5 out of every 100 occasions.

The fourth step is the performance of computation necessary for the test. The calculation includes testing statistics and the standard error. At this stage, it is worthwhile to bear in mind that when a hypothesis is tested there are four possibilities :

(i) The hypothesis is true but our test leads to its rejection.

(ii) The hypothesis is false but our test leads to its acceptance.

(iii) The hypothesis is true and our test leads to its acceptance.

(iv) The hypothesis is false and our test leads to its rejection.

Of these four possibilities, the first two lead to an erroneous decision. The first possibility leads to the Type-I error and the second possibility leads to the Type-II error.

The final step in hypothesis is to draw statistical decision involving the acceptance or rejection of hypothesis. This will depend on whether the computed value of the test falls in the region of acceptance or in the region of rejection at a given level of significance. If a hypothesis is tested at 5% level and the observed set has probabilities less than 5%, we consider that the difference between the sample statistics and hypothetical parameter is significant.

6. TESTING OF HYPOTHESIS – AN ILLUSTRATION

A researcher, who has undertaken research in management of small scale industry, has set up a hypothesis. 'Technical qualification of small entrepreneurs does not promote interrelationship between small scale units and large scale units.' (These two attributes, technical qualification and interrelationship are independent). The null hypothesis is that there is no association between the attributes under the study.

The Chi-square test is useful in cases of two independent samples. The value of x^2 is the measure that expresses the extent of differences. Table 1 given below shows the relationship between technical qualification and inter-relationship.

TABLE 1

Technical Qualification of Small Entrepreneurs and Inter-relationship between Small Scale Units and Large Scale Units

TR / TQ	Low	Medium	Total
TQ	3	21	24
NTQ	8	13	21
Total	11	34	45

IR = Inter-relationship.
Low = Low Inter-relationship Units.
Medium = Medium Inter-relationship Units.
TQ = Technically Qualified Entrepreneurs.
NTQ = Not Technically Qualified Entrepreneurs.

In order to see whether there is any co-relation between technical qualification and inter-relationship x^2 test has been computed.

TABLE 2

Technical Qualification of Entrepreneur of Small Scale Units and Interrelationship : Chi-square Test

Cell	*fe*	*f*	*f-fe*	*(f-fe)*^{2}	$\frac{(f-fe)^2}{fe}$
R_1 Col 1	5,866	3	2,866	8.217	1.400
R_1 Col 2	18,133	21	–2,866	8.217	0.453
R_2 Col 1	5,133	8	–2,867	0.219	1.601
R_2 Col 1	15,886	13	2,866	8.217	1.517
				Total	4.971

Table 2 indicates that the calculated chi-square value is more than the Table chi-square value at 5% level. Therefore, the chi-square test also reveals that there is significant co-relation between technical qualification and interrelationship of small and large scale units. The hypotheses that technical qualification promotes interrelationship is accepted.

The objectives of the study and the hypotheses to be examined should be clearly stated and agreed upon at the outset. These objectives and hypothesis shape and mould the study; they determine the kind of information that is required, the specific data that are to be collected, and the kind of analysis that will be necessary. The hypothesis makes the study more scientific and useful for decision making.

CHAPTER EIGHT
SAMPLING

1. *Sampling*
2. *Sampling – A Common Activity*
3. *Advantages of Sampling*
4. *Limitations of Sampling*
5. *Theoretical Basis of Sampling*
6. *Steps in Sampling*
7. *Probability Sampling*
8. *Non-Probability Sampling*
9. *Sampling Error*
10. *Non-Sampling Error*

1. SAMPLING

1.1 INTRODUCTION

Data originally collected for an investigation are known as primary data. Such data are original in character. The primary data may be collected by following either census method or the sampling method.

Under the census method data are collected from each and every unit of the universe. If one is interested in learning more about foreign cars in Tamil Nadu the universe will comprise the total number of foreign cars. The universe may be person, household, shop, field, factory, university and the like.

Sampling method is the process of learning about the population on the basis of a sample. Sample is that part of the universe which we select for the purpose of investigation. A sample should exhibit the characteristics of the universe. It should be a microsome a word which literally means 'Small Universe'.

Paul L. Erdos and Arthur J. Morgan define a sample thus : "Statistical Sampling may be defined as a process of selecting a segment of the universe to obtain information of ascertainable reliability about the population." (Erdos and Morgan, 1970, p. 31).

Blalock and Blalock define a sample as "It is a small piece of the population obtained by a probability process that mirrors, with known precision, the various patterns and sub-classes of the population." (Hubert M. Blalock Jr. and Ann B. Blalock, 1968, p. 297).

2. SAMPLING — A COMMON ACTIVITY

Sampling is an essential part of all scientific procedures. It is well developed in biological researches, physics, chemistry and social sciences.

Before deciding the method of collection of data choosing from experimentation, observation, interview and mail survey, the researcher has to decide whether he wants to collect data from every unit of the universe or whether he will use only a portion of the universe.

Sampling is a common activity in our day to day life. We submit to blood tests as part of physical examination since few drops we surrender can give a lot of information about our health.

A housewife tests a few grains of rice at the boiling point to find out whether the rice is fully cooked or not. A teacher asks a few students some questions to test whether the students are well informed in a particular subject or not. In the morning we test the warmth of our coffee by taking a sip. Everyday newspapers report the results of studies. The public opinion on such studies is estimated by collecting opinions from few selected individuals. In all such cases by studying the sample we seek to know the universe or population.

3. ADVANTAGES OF SAMPLING

The following advantages make sampling a desirable method of obtaining information.

1. Information is collected from only a portion of the population. It is less costlier to survey a sample of 150 people than to survey a population of 15,000 people.
2. The data can be collected and summarised more quickly. The results are available quickly and so decisions could be taken without much delay.

3. Sampling gives scope for more accurate data. The researcher can concentrate on the sample and make a thorough probing. The researcher cannot discharge his work with that level of diligence as is required in dealing with a large population.
4. It is possible for the researcher to collect more elaborate information from the few sample units than from the large population. Collection of data from all units leads to administrative problems and therefore in depth study becomes difficult.
5. When the universe is extremely large, it will be very difficult to study every unit of the universe. Hence sampling is the only practical method for collection of data.
6. Sampling is indispensable when the study results in spoiling the element sampled. A company making electric lamps can not test every one of them with respect to its maximum life or life voltage resistance, since nothing will be left to be sold.

4. LIMITATIONS OF SAMPLING

The sampling method is not free from limitations. They are:

1. Sampling is not feasible in any situation where precise knowledge about each unit of the population is needed. A public utility company supplying electricity can not bill their individual consumers on the basis of an average drawn from a sample of electricity consumers.
2. The accuracy and realiability of sample data is affected by two different types of errors — sampling errors and data collection errors.
3. In a census survey it may be easy to check the omissions of certain units in view of complete coverage. But this is not possible in the case of a sample survey.

5. THEORETICAL BASIS OF SAMPLING

Sampling is a process of taking a few units from a target population, analysing the sample data and making conclusion about the population. With the help of probability sampling estimate of population mean or other parameter can be made with considerable precision. The branch of statistics dealing with this activity is called sampling theory.

There are two important laws on which the theory of sampling is based :

1. Law of Statistical Regularity and
2. Law of Inertia of Large Numbers.

The law of statistical regularity is derived from the mathematical theory of probability. In the words of King "Law of Statistical Regularity lays down that a moderately large number of items chosen at random from a large group are almost sure on the average to possess the characteristics of the large group." (S.P. Gupta 1982, P.E. 4.4). This law emphasises that sample units must be selected at random.

The law of Inertia of large number states that other things being equal, the larger the size of the sample, the more accurate the results are likely to be. This is because large numbers are more stable as compared to small ones.

6. STEPS IN SAMPLING

There are six steps which precede collection of the data by means of sample.

The first step is defining the population or universe. The population or universe is the specific group of items which the researchers wish to study and about which they plan to generalise. If a theatre owner is investigating the movie going habits of a local college students, the population will be the students enrolled on a particular date. The definition of the universe, in any particular case is determined solely by the research objectives of the particular study.

The second step is the development of a frame. A frame is a list of the population. It consists of names and addresses of the individuals and institutions. It can also specify a definite location, boundary, an address or a set of rules by which sampling unit can be identified. For example, a researcher has undertaken a study for finding the proportion of the grocery stores in the Madras metropolitan area, which stock cardamom. Here grocery stores would be observed. For the purpose of identifying the stores, a list of all Madras metropolitan area grocery stores must be obtained. From the list it will be easy to choose. If no such list is available one may choose a sample of areas.

The third step is the selection of sample design. The researcher can go for probability or non-probability design. If the researcher wants to estimate the sampling error of the results, a probability sample should be used. If it is very difficult to develop a frame, a non-probability sample should be used. The researcher should feel confident that the sample used provides a legitimate and accurate picture of the universe.

The fourth step is selecting the sample size. The sample size should never be less than thirty. The sample size should be around one-tenth of the size of population. But the final decision on proper sample size really depends on whether the researcher feels reasonably confident that his sample is large enough to accurately depict the population.

The fifth step is the selection of substitute sample units. All the units selected for the sample will not participate. This necessitates the substitution of sample members for non-respondents.

The final step is cost consideration. The size and type of sample as well as the data collection method depend upon cost considerations. Probability sample surveys incur callback costs, listing costs, and variety of other costs. The non-probability sample can be used with less cost.

7. PROBABILITY SAMPLING

There are two types of sampling-probability sampling and non-probability sampling. In probability sampling each unit of the universe has a known chance of being selected. In probability sampling design, the population must be clearly defined and the list of target population must be available. The most frequently used probability sampling methods are discussed below.

7.1 SIMPLE RANDOM SAMPLING

In this sampling each unit of the universe has been known and has equal chance of being selected. The tools used for selection are lots or random numbers.

In the latter method the universe is listed. Each unit of the universe is given a serial number. The numbers are written on pieces of paper and folded. All the papers are pooled and shuffled and then lots are drawn to choose the required number. Instead of pieces of paper, plastic discs or coins can also be used. This method is suitable for drawing small number of samples from a small universe. The following example will illustrate this method clearly. If we want to take a sample of 10 persons out of a population of 100 persons the procedure is to write the names of all the 100 persons on separate slips of paper, fold these slips, mix them thoroughly, and then make a blindfold selection of 10 slips.

The random numbers are quite suitable if the size of the population is large. Statisticians have framed random numbers for large samples out of large populations. A researcher wants to select 250 workers from a factory with a labour force of 5,000. The workers on the list could be numbered and then random number could be used to make the selection. For framing the random numbers, we shall number each unit from 1 to 5,000. Then we open a page of Tippett's numbers (Tippett's 1927) random number tables consist of 41,600 random digits grouped into 10,400 sets of four digit random numbers and select first 250 numbers. The selected 250 persons will be included in the sample.

The selection of sample by random numbers is laborious. An alternative is simply to calculate the desired sampling fraction (total population divided by desired number of samples) and select every kth worker throughout the list, starting with a randomly chosen number between 1 and k inclusive. K = N/n. Here the population (N) consists of 5000 workers and the number of sample members to be selected (n) are 250 members. Therefore $K = \frac{5000}{250} = 20$. A number between 1 and 20 is selected at random and this determines the first sample number. If this number is 6, the sample is composed of the numbers 6, 26, 46, 66, and so on. The procedure is easy and convenient.

Another way of simple random sampling is the selection from sequential list. Under this system, names are first arranged serially according to some particular order, which maybe alphabetical, geographical or simply serial. Then out of the list, every 10th or any other number of the case may be taken up. A beginning may be made from the middle. The selection may begin from 7th, 17th, 27th, and 37th numbers.

Yet another simple random sampling is grid system. According to this method, a map of entire area is prepared. Then a screen with square is placed upon the map. Some of the squares are selected at random. The areas falling within the selected squares are taken as samples.

7.2 SYSTEMATIC SAMPLING

This method is used, when the complete list of population is available. The researcher first has to arrange the units of the universe on some basis say alphabetically, chronologically, geographically, ascending order of capital employed or number of persons employed or descending order of capital employed or labour employed. Secondly he has to decide the number of samples to be taken out of the population. Thirdly calculate N/n (N indicates the universe and n represents sample). If the population is 100, the sample to be selected is 10, N is $\frac{100}{10} = 10$. Fourthly select the first item at random using the lottery method within the interval. Lastly every N/nth unit from the first sample will be included in the sample.

The following illustration makes this technique very clear. Suppose the company Honesty Limited wants to determine the attitude of their white collar employees towards the existing fringe benefits. Assume that there are 2000 employees working in Honesty Limited. The researcher wants to select the sample. He arranges the names of employees alphabetically and decides to select 40 employees. Afterwards he calculates N/n, i.e., $\frac{2000}{40} = 50$. The calculation reveals that out of every 50 persons one has to be selected. He then, by casting lots selects one person between 1 and 50. The seventh person has been selected at random. He then selects every 50th person after seven. Thus he selects from the list of names the 7th, 57th, 107th, 157th etc.

The systematic sample is simple and convenient and it requires only less time and work.

The limitation of this method of sampling is that there will be a bias in the results. Suppose a researcher wants to study the influence of technical qualification on the attitude of employees towards the management, this sampling technique has limited use. With the help of this sampling technique 8th, 58th, 108th... 508th employees will be selected. The sample consists of only employees with technical qualification. This method of sampling is not suitable for heterogenous population.

7.3 STRATIFIED SAMPLING

If the researcher is interested in certain groups within the total population, then the universe is divided into strata on the basis of some measurable criterion such as age, income, education and the like. The steps involved in stratification are the following.

1. Decide the basis of stratification.
2. Decide the number of strata.
3. Stratify the population according to the criterion.
4. Decide the size of the sample in each stratum.

The following example illustrates the technique of stratified sampling. A researcher wants to study the attitude of the employees of Little Company Limited towards the fringe benefits. The workers' attitudes on this subject are closely tied to their age. Younger workers are less concerned about fringe benefits than the older workers. In this case a stratified sample could be used. The workers can be classified into four groups say workers less than 25 years of age, in the age group of 25-40, 41-55 and more than 55 years of age. Then the researcher has to decide the size of the sample in each stratum. There is no rule that the size of the sample in each stratum should be equal. The researcher can decide on equal size or proportionate size.

7.4 PROPORTIONATE STRATIFIED SAMPLING

The number of units in each stratum is proportionate to its number in the universe. The following table illustrates proportionate stratified sampling.

Classification of Workers According to their Age

Category	*Total*	*Percentage to Total*	*Number in Sample*
Less than 25 years of age	250	10	25
25-40 years of age	1250	50	125
41-55 years of age	825	33	82
More than 55 years of age	175	7	18
Total	2500	100	250

The break up of workers shows that the number of sample workers has been selected in proportion to size of the population.

If equal number of units are drawn from each stratum regardless of the size of the strata the sampling is called disproportionate stratified sampling.

7.5 CLUSTER SAMPLING

In this sampling the various units comprising the population are grouped in clusters and the sample selection is made in such a way that each cluster has an equal chance of being drawn. It applies to different units of study such as products, people and geographical areas.

Suppose a survey is to be done in a large town and that the unit of enquiry is individual household. Further, the town contains 20,000 households and a sample of 200 households is to be selected. One way would be to pick 200 households from the entire population by some random method. This would spread the sample over the whole town and cost of field work would be high.

With a view to concentrate the sample in a few parts of the town, the town is divided into 400 areas with 50 households in each. At random 4 areas (i.e., 1 in 100) would be selected and the study would include all the households in the sample. The overall probability of selection is unchanged but, by selecting clusters of households, one has materially simplified and cheapened the fieldwork of the survey.

There are three general points to be noted about cluster sapling :

First "whether or not a particular aggregate of units should be called a cluster depends on circumstances." (Moser and Kalton, 1974, p.101). If areas are taken as clusters, households become individual units. If households are taken as a cluster, the members of the households become individual units.

Secondly clusters need not always be natural aggregates such as localities, schools, colleges and classes. Artificial clusters may be formed by imposing grids into maps. More commonly, clustering takes advantage of existing groupings of the population. The clusters do not usually contain equal numbers.

Thirdly in any one sample several levels of clusters may be used. For example, if a researcher wants to study working conditions of agricultural labourers in a state, the first level will be various districts, second taluks, third revenue villages and finally villages.

The merit of cluster sampling is that it lowers the field costs. Another advantage of cluster sampling is that it is being used when no satisfactory sampling frame for the whole population exists.

The major limitation of cluster sampling is the similarity of one unit in the cluster with its other units.

7.6 AREA SAMPLING

In this method the area to be covered by a survey is divided into a number of smaller areas, of which a sample is selected by random. Within these areas, either a complete enumeration is carried out or a further sub-sample is taken.

Suppose a survey of living conditions is to be made in a sample of dwellings in a town, the town area is then divided into blocks. The boundaries of the blocks must be well-defined and easily identifiable by the field-workers. The blocks must be stratified and assigned measures of size. Then the selection of primary units from each stratum by following random method must be done. Finally sub-sample of small units within each stratum or complete enumeration of households will be carried out.

7.7 MULTI-PHASE SAMPLING

Multi-phase sampling is a type of sample design in which some information is collected from the whole sample and additional information is collected either at the same time or later from sub-sample of the full sample. For example, in a survey of selected sample households, one can question them on all matters such as size, composition of the households, occupation of its heads and income. Some information may be collected from only a small part of the entire sample.

Multi-phase sampling is used to estimate the effect of non-response in the sub-sample. The multi-phase sampling increases the precision of sub-sample results. The cost of first phase sample is cheaper than the second phase, since the first-phase information is taken from some records or collected by mail questionnaires while the second phase information is obtained by personal interviews.

7.8 REPLICATED SAMPLING

In replicated sampling, several random sub-samples are selected from the population instead of one full sample. All the sub-samples have the same design and each one of them is a self-contained sample of the population.

Under this method the population is first divided into as many zones as there are sample units to be included in each sub-sample. For example, if we want to draw five sub-samples of 10 employees each from a total of 400 employees, each of the five sub-samples will be formed either by reading out 10 random numbers—one from each zone or by reading out one random number in the first zone only and then systematically selecting every 40th unit thereafter.

With replicated sampling, sampling estimates can be calculated for each of the sub-samples and the variation between these estimates can be assessed. It was first introduced by Mahal Nobis in 1936.

Replicated sampling helps to find out non-sampling errors. Each of the sub-samples produces an independent estimate of the population characteristics. Each of the sub-samples is interviewed by different interviewer or set of interviewers. Each estimate shows the difference between interviewer variation.

There are two main disadvantages of replicated sampling. Firstly replicated would not be helpful in undertaking a detailed investigation of bias as the numbers in the separate sub-samples tend to be small. Secondly replicated sampling is costlier as personal interviews and processing of data would be higher in cost than that of the single large sample.

8. NON-PROBABILITY SAMPLING

In this sampling method, each unit of the population does not have equal chance of being selected. An estimate of the sampling error cannot be made.

8.1 JUDGMENT OR PURPOSIVE SAMPLING

In this method samples are taken based on the judgment of the researcher. A super market authority wants to study the attitude of customers of ice cream section. the researcher feels that the greatest users of this service are school children. He also knows that most of these children shop on Sundays. thus he interviews only the Sunday shoppers. In this sampling he includes those people whom he wants to include.

8.2 CONVENIENCE SAMPLING

Under this method, the units are selected according to the conveniences of the researcher such as nearness, easy availability of data, etc. For example, if a sample of 50 adults from the city of Coimbatore are to be interviewed, the investigator goes to some location in Coimbatore say Peelamedu and selects each person crossing a particular spot at 10 minutes' intervals.

This method is mostly used for pilot study, which is being undertaken for getting insight into the subject matter of study.

8.3 QUOTA SAMPLING

This sampling method is similar to the stratified sampling method. The universe is divided into strata on the basis of certain characteristics. Then the quota is fixed for each stratum in proportion to the size. The investigator chooses the units in each strata in a non-random manner. For example, a researcher wants to study the attitude of employees of Super Company Limited towards fringe benefits. Out of the total 2500 employees, 250 (10%) are in the age group of less than 25 years, 1250 (50%) belong to 25-40 years, 825 (33%) belong to 41-55 years, and 175 (7%) belong to more than 55 years of age. In the first stratum the researcher will have to select 25 employees (10% of 250). In quota sampling the researcher will select any 25 persons according to his convenience.

8.4 SNOWBALL SAMPLING

This refers to a form of sampling in which the researcher first finds a few subjects, who are characterised by the qualities the investigator seeks and interviews them. He then asks them for names of other people whom they know and have the same qualities or other qualities. In this manner, the investigator accumulates more and more respondents. There is no sampling frame listing of all those who are going to be included in a study.

For example, if the investigator was able to find a few bonded labourers willing to talk to him he might ask them for the names and locations of others; who might also be willing to be interviewed.

Sampling of this type has often been done in studies for elite groups, either those in power in a community or members of upper classes. In community studies there is often the feeling that only those in power really know who else has power.

9. SAMPLING ERROR

The discrepancy in the inferences about the population on the basis of few observations (sampling) and the population is called sampling error. The results derived from a sample study may not be exactly equal to the true value in the population. These errors would not be present in a complete enumeration survey. Sampling errors are of two types — biased errors and unbiased errors.

Biased errors arise from any bias in selection and collection information and faulty method of analysis. The use of non-random sampling in the place of random sampling, substitution of an item in the place of one chosen in a random sample, non-response to all items in the questionnaire, appeal to the vanity of the person questioned, securing inadequate frame, poorly designed questionnaire, ill-trained interviewer, bias in the flow of the data and faulty process of selection are some of the reasons responsible for bias.

The unbiased errors arise due to chance differences between the members of the population. The estimate obtained from a particular sample will differ from the universe value, because the sample selected by chance is not truly representative of the universe. If the researcher took another random sample from the same universe, the resulting estimate might differ a little.

There are two methods of reducing sampling error-avoidance of bias and increasing the size of the sample.

The law of statistical regularity points out that if a sample is taken at random from a population, it is likely to possess almost the same characteristics as that of the population.

The law of inertia of large numbers states that other things being equal, the larger the size of the sample, the more accurate the results are likely to be. This is because large numbers are more stable as compared to small ones.

10. NON-SAMPLING ERRORS

the results of the complete enumeration of units in the universe is also not free from error. Non-sampling error can occur at every stage of planning and execution of the census or survey. Non-sampling errors occur from one or more of the following factors.

1. Data collected may be inconsistent with respect to the objectives of the study.
2. Inappropriate methods of interview or observation.
3. Lack of trained and experienced investigators.
4. Lack of adequate inspection and supervision.
5. Errors due to non-response.
6. Errors in coding, punching and verification and
7. Errors committed during presentation and printing of tabulated results.

CHAPTER NINE
SCALING TECHNIQUES

1. INTRODUCTION

The entrance examination conducted measures the students' potential for college level work. A teacher counts the number of students in a class, classifies them as male or female and judges their personality. The teacher is involved in the process of measurement. A businessman engaged in marketing the product is interested in measuring the market potential for a new product, buyer's attitude, perceptions or preferences towards a new brand. This measurement process gives scope for providing meaningful information for decision making.

Measurement may be defined as the assignment of numbers to characteristics of objects or events according to rules. It is important to note that it is the characteristics of objects or events that are measured and not the objects or events themselves. For example, we can measure buyer's preference, income and attitude and product's sweetness, size, colour and speed.

There are four characteristics of the number system 0, 1, 2, 3, 4, 5, 6, 7, 8 and 9. First each number in the series is unique and there are ten numbers. Second the ordering of the numbers is given by convention (e.g.) 1,2,3 and so on. Third we can define equal differences.

(e.g.) 3-2 = 7-6
1 = 1
7-5 = 3-1
2 = 2

Fourth we can define equal ratios (e.g.) 10 – 5 = 6 – 3
2 = 2

2. MEASUREMENT SCALES

Scale is a yardstick like any instrument for finding length, weight, volume and the like. The scale does not possess the properties associated with most physical measures. The scales can be generally classified into following major categories.

(1) Nominal scale;

(2) Ordinal scale;

(3) Interval scale;and

(4) Ratio scale.

2.1 NOMINAL SCALE

In nominal scale, numbers are used to identify or categorise objects or events. For example, the population of a town may be classified according to sex into "males" and "females" or according to religion into "Hindus", "Muslims" "Sikhs" and "Christians".

In Marketing Research nominal scales are needed to measure brands, store types, sales territories, geographical locations, heavy versus light users, working versus non-working women and brand awareness versus non-awareness.

The following illustration gives an idea regarding the use of nominal scale.

Reasons for Purchase by Sex

Reasons for Purchase	*Male*		*Female*		*Total*	
	No	*Per cent*	*No*	*Per cent*	*No*	*Per cent*
Weight	10	20	28	56	38	38
Speed	31	62	10	20	41	41
Miscellaneous	9	18	12	24	21	21
Total	50	100	50	100	100	100

As it could be seen from the illustration, males are concerned with speed and females are concerned with weight.

Nominal scales can be developed from a response to a question. Does your car have Chakara Tyres? The responses may be Yes, No and Don't know. For nominally scaled data, statistical analysis such as mode, percentages, the binomial test and chi-square test can be used. A mean or median cannot be calculated.

2.2 ORDINAL SCALE

The ordinal scale indicates the relative position of two or more objects or some characteristics. The consumers are asked to rank preferences for several brands, flavours or package designs. The measures of such preference are ordinal in nature. One may rank two or more households according to their annual income. Suppose we have five households with annual incomes as shown below :

	Households				
	A	*B*	*C*	*D*	*E*
Annual Income (Rs.)	6,000	10,000	4,800	12,000	11,000

The household with highest income is given No.1 and the next to it No.2 and so on; then the following order will emerge.

Households	*Order of households on the basis of annual income*
A	IV
B	III
C	V
D	I
E	II

The marketing data involves ordinal measurement. Most data collected by the process of interrogation have ordinal properties. For example, the measurement of attitude, opinion preference and perception involves 'greater than' or 'less than' judgements.

2.3 INTERVAL SCALE

The interval scale has all characteristics of the ordinal scale and in addition, the units of measure or intervals between successive positions are equal.

For example, a researcher scaled brands A, B and C on an interval scale regarding the buyers' degree of liking of the brands. Brand A receives the highest liking score of 6, B receives 3 and C receives 2. First the liking for brand A is more favourable than that for brand B. Second the degree of liking between A and B is three times greater than the liking between B and C.

The statistical tools used to analyse the interval data are range, mean, standard deviation and the like. Interval scales are frequently used in commercial marketing research studies, especially in collecting attitudinal and overall brand rating information.

2.4 RATIO SCALES

The ratio scales have all the properties of nominal scale, ordinal scale and interval scale. They have order, distance and unique origin. Once a ratio scale has been established, its value can be transformed only by multiplying each value by a constant. Thus, on a ratio scale, a score of 90 is twice that of 45.

Ratio scales are found more commonly used in the physical sciences than in the social sciences. Measures of weight, length, time intervals, area, velocity etc. all conform to ratio scales. In social sciences, we do find properties of concern that can be ratio scaled; money, age, years of education, etc. all confirm to ratio scales. However, successful ratio scaling of behavioural attributes is rare.

3. RELIABILITY AND VALIDITY

There are two important criteria for ascertaining whether the scale developed is good or not. These are reliability and validity.

3.1 RELIABILITY

Reliability denotes stability and consistency. The reliability of a measure is its capacity to yield the same results in repeated applications to the same events. There are various types of errors which reduce the reliability of a measure. There are different methods of measuring reliability test such as (1) Test – retest (2) split – half (3) multiple parallel or alternative form.

In the 'test-retest' method, the same measure is applied twice to the same individuals at two different points and the resulting scores correlated. The higher the co-efficient of correlation the higher is the reliability of the measure. This method is best suited to study the characteristics of the human beings.

Under split-half method a large pool of questions or statements is split into two sub-measures. The technique of spliting a measure is to create a sub-measure using odd number and another sub-measure using even numbered items. Both the sub-measures are administered to the respondents during the same interview. The scores on the two sub-measures are then correlated and this co-efficient called the co-efficient of internal consistency is taken as a measure of reliability.

In multiple, parallel or alternative method, two forms of a measure are administered to the same individuals. Both forms include questions or statements measuring the same concept but worded differently. The spacing of these administrations varies from study to study. In some cases the two forms are administered in the same session. In other cases, several months may pass between administering the two forms. In the final step, the results of these two forms are correlated to determine the degree of reliability.

The multiple forms are used when it is intended to determine the impact of a certain change programme, e.g., a programme to increase knowledge, change attitudes, alter values and the like.

3.2 VALIDITY

Validity of a measure refers to the extent to which the measurement process is free from both systematic and random errors.

The systematic error causes a constant bias in the measurements. For example, we are measuring the speed of events at a swimming meet, using a stop watch, which systematically runs fast. The swimming speeds measured will cause an upward bias.

For a measure to be valid it must be reliable. Here systematic error(s) and random error(s) are zero. If a measure is not reliable it can not be valid. If it is reliable it may or may not be valid. Consequently, validity of a measure is of main concern since it deals with both systematic and random errors.

An easy measure of validity would be to compare the observed measurement with the true measure. Rarely we know the true measure. Consequently we infer the validity of the observed measurement by using one or more estimation methods. The major ways to estimate the validity of measurement are: *(i)* Construct validity *(ii)* Content Validity *(iii)* Concurrent Validity and *(iv)* Predictive Validity.

Construct validity involves the understanding of the theoretical rationale underlying the obtained measurements. For example, a sales manager believes that there is a relationship between job satisfaction and job performance of a sales force. Construct validity could be assessed by developing measures of theses two constructs and ascertaining the relationship among the measures for a group of sales personnel. Those who have high job satisfaction should exhibit high job performance scores. If they do not we could question the construct validity of the measures or validity of the hypothesised relationship.

Content validity involves a subjective judgement by an expert or experts as to the appropriateness of the measurement. This is a common method used in marketing research. For example, a marketing researcher is going to measure 'the image of retail stores in a grocery chain'. He develops a questionnaire consisting of 20 questions. These 20 questions have been used to build an index for measuring the image. The validity of these 20 items would be determined by having an expert or experts.

Concurrent validity involves correlating the two different measurements of marketing phenomenon, which have been administered at the same point of time. It is primarily used to determine the validity of new measuring techniques by correlating them with established techniques.

For example, the personality of the sales persons are measured with the help of scoring scheme. Alternatively another measurement is proposed. Concurrent validation would involve administering both techniques under identical conditions and correlating the two measures measuring the personality of the sales persons. A high correlation would establish the concurrent validity of the new techniques.

Predictive validity involves the ability of a measured marketing phenomenon at one point of time to predict another marketing phenomenon at a future point of time. For example, the scholastic aptitude test is used to measure the student's aptitude for college-level work. This is used as a predictor of future performance of students in college.

4. ATTITUDE SCALING

Attitude is learned predisposition to respond in a consistently favourable or unfavourable manner with respect to a given object. (Fishbein and Ajzen 1975, p. 6) Attitude represents a person's evaluation of an object, based upon the person's belief about that object, and, to some degree attitudes determine how the person will respond to the object in the future. The concept of attitude is generally viewed as being structured into three interrelated components; cognitions (belief) affect (feelings) and conation (bebavioural intentions).

Attitude can be measured directly by asking questions as to how he feels about an object. The other alternative methods are observation of behaviour, indirect techniques such as word association tests, sentence completion tests, story-telling, performance of objective tasks and psychological reactions. Since the self report method of attitude measurement is most frequently used, the discussion here is based primarily on it.

There are three steps involved in attitude measurement. First one should develop a set of statements relating to the subject of enquiry. Such statements should be simple, precise and unambiguous. The statements should be written in simple language so that the respondent easily understands them.

The second step is to choose the statements to be included in the final scale. For this purpose, a pilot study is undertaken in which some persons are asked to respond to all statements. In the light of such study some statements may be eliminated or modified. Another approach is to ask a group of judges to assess the suitability of items for the final scale.

Finally, the scale, once formed should be tested for its reliability and validity. If the scale satisfies these criteria it can be used in the survey.

A scale may be composed of indicators representing multi-dimension or unidimension of a concept. The former is multidimentional scale and the latter is called to construct a new scale or adopt an already constructed scale, he should understand how it was made. If he does not, he is likely to use it inaccurately and may find interpreting the results very difficult.

4.1 LIKERT SCALE

The most widely used form of scaling in survey research is Likert scale. It sets up ordinal categories for degrees of agreement, generally including the five levels of Strongly Agree, Disagree, Strongly Disagree and Don't Know. These response categories are attached to a set of statements. Assuming that the responses to each statement are equivalent, you can assign scores of 1 through 5 (or 0 through 4) and create an index by summing up the scores. In respect of negatively worded statements this scoring is reversed.

The procedure used to construct a Likert type scale is summarised as follows :

(i) A number of statements believed to be relevant to the attitude being measured are collected and classified either "favourable" or "unfavourable". Items that appear to be neutral are omitted.

(ii) A pretest is conducted in which a group of respondents indicate their opinions of each item according to one of the response categories presented.

(iii) Each response is given a numerical score (for example +2, +1, 0, –1, –2) based on a series of integers in arithmetic sequence. Scores are assigned in such a way that the direction of attitude (favourable to unfavourable) is consistent over all

items. For example, if a +2 is assigned to "Strongly agree" for faourable items, the same score is aligned to "strongly disagree" for unfavourable items.

(iv) Each respondent's total is obtained by adding his item scores.

(v) Items to be included in the final test are determined by analysing the results of the pretest. The correlation between statement scores and the total scores is then ascertained. Those statements which have a high correlation with the total scores are then selected for the final test.

(vi) The final test is administered to the group of respondents of interest and is scored in the same way as in the pretest.

The Likert type scale has certain advantages over the Thurstone differential scale. First, the procedure is such that it is simpler to construct. Second, the Likert-scale provides for expression of intensity of feeling. Third, this scale appears to be more reliable.

4.2 SEMANTIC DIFFERENTIAL SCALE

This scale was developed initially by Osgood, Suci and Tannenbaum (1957). A semantic Differential scale offers bipolar positions (such as two adjectives : active/passive) to a single stimulus (for example : My Mother).

The technique has been used in too many ways and for too many purposes. Some of the major uses have been to compare company images and brands, determine attitudinal characteristics of consumers and analyse the effectiveness of promotional activities. The semantic differential is a technique for measuring the psychological meaning of things usually concepts or objects or people to individuals or group of people. Thus one object can be presented to a group of people or the individuals could be asked to rate more than one object. The semantic differential consists of a series or set of descriptive polar opposite rating scales, each assumed to be an equal-interval ordinal scale. The scale can have any number of positions, although usually it is an odd-numbered position scale, generally seven-point.

For example, to measure reactions to a new type of shaving cream, the management had asked its men to use the shaving cream in their home for one week. At the end of the week the men were given a ten-item semantic differential scale used. Six of the scales were thought to reflect valuative meaning "likable-unlikable" "good-bad", "pleasant-unpleasant", "useful-useless", "beneficial-harmful" and "attractive-unattractive". The attitude towards shaving with the new type of shaving cream would be calculated by summing up individual's responses to the six items shown in the following table.

Semantic differential scale in my opinion, the shaving experience using shaving cream

Likable	–	–	–	–	–	–	–	–	Unlikable
Good	–	–	–	–	–	–	–	–	Bad
Cold	–	–	–	–	–	–	–	–	Hot
Unpleasant	–	–	–	–	–	–	–	–	Pleasant
Sharp	–	–	–	–	–	–	–	–	Dull
Useful	–	–	–	–	–	–	–	–	Useless
Boring	–	–	–	–	–	–	–	–	Interesting
Beneficial	–	–	–	–	–	–	–	–	Harmful
Attractive	–	–	–	–	–	–	–	–	Unattractive
Active	–	–	–	–	–	–	–	–	Passive

4.3 THURSTONE SCALE

Thurstone scale is one of the earliest and best known forms of scaling. The steps to be followed for the construction of the scale are the following :

First a large number of statements pertaining to the subject of enquiry are collected. The various methods such as literature survey, personal experience and discussion with knowledgeable persons are followed for developing statements. These statements should range from one extreme of favourable attitude to the other extreme of unfavourable attitude.

Second is the selection of the statements. Thurstone and Chave have given five criteria for selecting the statements. These are: *(i)* The statements should be brief. *(ii)* They should be such that can be accepted or rejected in accordance with the attitude of the respondent. *(iii)* The acceptance or rejection of the statement should indicate the respondent's attitude. *(iv)* Ambiguous double-barrelled statements must be avoided and *(v)* The statements must be related to attitude.

On the basis of the above procedure, the researcher selects some 20 to 30 statements. The scale values are equally spaced. The selected statements are embodied in a questionnaire. They are included in a random order so that there is no hierarchy of scale values. The questionnaire is administered and the respondent is asked to endorse all those statements with which he agrees. The average of the scale values of all the statements he endorses becomes his total scores.

4.4 GUTTMAN SCALES

The construction of a Guttam scale starts out by defining the total attitude being scaled. A sample of items representing the universe is selected for possible inclusion in the scale. These items are administered to a sample of persons. Then the responses are subjected to what is called scalogram analysis to test the scalability of items. This is meant in the technical sense that the questions should belong to the same attitude dimension.

For example, to test the 'Arithmetical ability' the following five problems are ordered in terms of difficulty.

(1) $3 + 4 =$

(2) $29 + 37 =$

(3) $47 + 59 - 17 =$

(4) $(33 + 17) - 15 =$

(5) $(46 \times 15) - (26 - 19 + 3) =$

Any one who obtains correct answer to problem (5) will also get problems (1) to (4) right, anyone who gets (4) right will get problems (1) to (3) right etc. Thus we might anticipate only six patterns of answers (assuming no one makes a slip), which may be set out as follows (with a 'X' indicating the correct answer and '-' not the correct answer).

Problems

(1)	*(2)*	*(3)*	*(4)*	*(5)*	*Score*
+	+	+	+	+	5
+	+	+	+	–	4
+	+	+	–	–	3
+	+	–	–	–	2
+	–	–	–	–	1
–	–	–	–	–	0

A diagram in which the individuals' responses are laid out as above is called a scalogram. If a set of 'n' attitude items is perfectly scaleable in the above sense, the scalogram contains only (n + 1) response patterns, which are known as scale types. One can infer from the individual's total score precisely which items he agreed and disagreed with.

Now let us discuss an important characteristic of an unidimensional scale. Assume that there are five attitude statements ranging from the most favourable to the least with respect to some psychological aspects. We rank these statements, in such a manner that the most favourble statement is assigned rank 1, The next most favourable rank 2 and so on, with the least favourable statement standing at rank 5. Assume that there are five respondents whose attitude we want to measure. Each respondent is asked whether he agrees with the statements or not. If he agrees with the statement he is given a weight of 1 and if he disagrees he is assigned a weight of 0. If we assume that the attitude statements fall along an unidimensional continuum and the responses of the individuals to the statements are determined only by their position on the same continuum the position is shown below :

Scores and Ranks of Respondents

Respondents	*1 2 3 4 5*	*Scores of Respondents*	*Ranks of Respondents*
A	1 1 1 1 1	5	1
B	0 1 1 1 1	4	2
C	0 0 1 1 1	3	3
D	0 0 0 1 1	2	4
E	0 0 0 0 1	1	5
F	0 0 0 0 0	0	6

The researcher would not know in advance whether a given set of attitude statements falls along an unidimensional continuum from the least to the most favourable.

5. A MODEL ATTITUDE SCALE

Attitude Scale Constructed to Measure the Attitude of Policyholders towards Postal Life Insurance Policies

Sl. No.	*Statements*	*Responses*				
		SA	*A*	*NO*	*DA*	*SDA*
1.	Premium rate is low	5	4	3	2	1
2.	Remittance of premium is more convenient	5	4	3	2	1
3.	Bonus on policies is high	5	4	3	2	1
4.	Policy document is received in time	5	4	3	2	1
5.	Customer service is good	5	4	3	2	1
6.	After sales service is attractive	5	4	3	2	1
7.	Post Office is situated near the residence	5	4	3	2	1
8.	Response to inquiries is prompt	5	4	3	2	1

9.	Document for tax purpose is given promptly	5	4	3	2	1
10.	Loan procedure is easy	5	4	3	2	1
11.	Settling the claims easily	5	4	3	2	1
12.	Surrender value is high	5	4	3	2	1
13.	On taking up PLI policies, social security gets improved	5	4	3	2	1
14.	Advertisement is appealing	5	4	3	2	1
15.	Risk is covered for any kind of death	5	4	3	2	1
16.	Number of premiums paid and the assured sum paid in case of death is very small.	5	4	3	2	1
17.	Nomination procedure is easy	5	4	3	2	1
18.	Procedure regarding lapse of policy is simple	5	4	3	2	1
19.	Revival of policy is easy	5	4	3	2	1
20.	Policy Assignment is easy	5	4	3	2	1
	Total	100	80	60	40	20

SA : Strongly Agree

A : Agree

NO : No Opinion (Neither Agree Nor Disagree)

DA : Disagree

SDA : Strongly Disagree

CHAPTER TEN

DATA PROCESSING

1. INTRODUCTION

The data that have been collected by following whatever method will be in the form of raw data. The first step in analysing that data will be to prepare these data for the type of analysis the researcher plans to carry out. Suppose an investigator collects data through observation and wants to write a paper, there is no need to convert them into quantifiable categories. An investigator wants to convert the raw data into numerical equivalents for the purposes of quantitative analyses and statistical testing, the data will be prepared to achieve the purpose.

The collected data must undergo some processing before analysis. The objectives of processing are the following :

1. Checking the questionnaires and schedules.
2. Reduction of mass data to manageable proportions.
3. Sum up the materials so as to prepare tables, charts and graphs and various groupings and breakdowns for presenting the results.
4. Minimising the errors which may creep in at various stages of the survey.

The processing of data involves activities such as editing, coding and tabulation.

2. EDITING

Editing means inspecting, correcting and modifying the collected data. The completed questionnaires returned from the field requires careful editing. Even the best interviewer is liable to make errors omit to ask questions, or to record answers. During the time of interview brief notes or symbols are used to record the data since it is very difficult to fill up the entire interview schedule. Editing is done at the time of collecting the data or later in the central office.

For a small survey, a single editor will assure maximum consistency of work. In bigger studies the task of editing may be broken down so that each editor can deal with all works of one section. Office editing is being followed when more than one interviewer collects data with the help of interview schedule or mailed questionnaires.

Before the questionnaire can be regarded as ready for coding, tabulation and analysis, it should be checked in the office for completeness, accuracy and uniformity.

2.1 COMPLETENESS

The editor must find whether there is an answer to every question. If the interviewer has forgotten to ask a question or to record the answer; it may be possible to deduce from other data on the questionnaire and fill up the gap. The interviewer may also be able to fill in the gap from his memory. If the information is vital, it can be collected by a postal enquiry.

Checking the completeness of the answers recorded for open questions is virtually impossible. If the data are not presented clearly, clarification cannot be obtained from the person who recorded it. To overcome this problem, tape recorder can be used at the time of interview.

2.2 ACCURACY

The editor must try to check whether the answers are accurate. In the first place, inconsistencies should be looked for. Every effort should be made to resolve clear inconsistencies. If this is not possible, then the inconsistent entries should be omitted.

2.3 UNIFORMITY

The editor must see whether the interviewers have interpreted questions and instructions uniformly. For example a question was asked How much per week the housewife spends on laundry? Some interviewers had mistakenly ringed the answer "under Rs.100/-" for housewives who did not send their clothes out for washing and pressing.

The investigator has to take into consideration the following basic problems before editing.

(*a*) Fictitious Interviews,

(*b*) Inconsistent replies,

(*c*) Incorrect answers,

(*d*) Incomplete answers and

(*e*) Don't know or 'No answer'.

The 'don't knows' usually fall into three categories. The are (*a*) legitimate don't knows (*b*) confused don't knows and (*c*) reluctant don't knows. Take the case of American pre-election voters' opinion in 1968 on two candidates, Mr. Nixon and Mr. Humphrey. Forty two per cent of voters expressed the hope that Mr. Humphrey will win the election. Forty five per cent of the voters favoured the candidature of Mr. Nixon and 13 per cent voters gave the opinion "Don't know". These don't knows will be distributed as follows :

$\frac{42}{87} \times 13$ to Mr. Humphery

$\frac{45}{87} \times 13$ to Mr. Nixon

The check in procedure is complex and complicated. After a questionnaire is received from the field, it must be inspected to determine whether it is acceptable for use in the study. Several problems relating to completeness and interviewing quality can cause a questionnaire to be excluded. The following aspects must be looked into.

(*i*) Portions of the questionnaire or key questions are left unanswered.

(*ii*) The respondent did not understand the instructions for filling out the questionnaire and/or did not take the task seriously.

(*iii*) The returned questionnaire may be physically incomplete, having a page or several pages missing.

(*iv*) The questionnaire may have been completed properly but returned after a pre-established cut off date.

A good editor must be not only intelligent, alert and experienced; he should also be rather conservative as to how to change an answer or complete one. He can consult the project director, who may discuss the problem with the ultimate user. When there is more than one editor, there must be an editor-in-chief who discusses all problems with the editors and incorporates the changes in the editing instructions.

3. CODING

The collected data have to be divided into meaningful categories. Categorisation is the process of using a set of rules to partition a body of data. The following four major rules guide the establishment of category sets. Categories should be :

3.1 APPROPRIATE TO THE RESEARCH PROBLEM

The number of categories should be reasonable. Generally 3 to 5 categories are considered reasonable. For example, categorisation of respondents on the basis of age, say, under 20 years, 20 to 29 years, 30 to 39 years and above 40 years may be relevant to the study.

3.2 EXHAUSTIVE

The rule on exhaustiveness states that there must be a category for every item. For example, there is a question in the questionnaire 'What is your favourite form of entertainment?'.

The alternatives will be:

Movies.

Skipping.

Boating.

Watching TV.

Other (describe)

For each question a separate number shall be assigned. For question 'Other' number 5 should be allotted. If majority has stated 'horse riding' allot the number 5 for that. If some say reading novels allot the number '6' to them.

3.3 MUTUALLY EXCLUSIVE

In an occupation survey the classification of respondents may be professional, managerial, sales, clerical, craftsman, operatives and unemployed. Some respondents will think of themselves as being in more than one of these groups. A man who views selling as profession may spend part of his time supervising others. He feels that he fits under three of these categories say professional, managerial and sales. One of the functions of operational definition is to provide categories.

3.4 SINGLE DIMENSION

Every class in the category set is defined in terms of one concept. In the example cited above, a respondent is both a salesman and unemployed. The 'salesman' label expresses the concept of occupational type while the response unemployed is another dimension.

Coding can be greatly simplified if precoded questionnaires are used. Enormous time is saved. When the possible answers anticipated, allot extra numbers when new categories emerge.

Coding is a laborious task. The problem can be kept to the minimum if preparations for coding are made prior to administering the questionnaire/interview schedule.

3.5 CODE SHEETS

Code sheets instruct the coders how to handle each question. When codes are defined, a listing of all types of responses being assigned to each code should be made on the code sheet. The code sheet consists of the following elements.

(i) Heading : The heading identifies the study.

(ii) Column identification : Each applicable column is to be listed on the left-hand side of the page.

(iii) Coding instructions : Limitations/restrictions and required multiple codes are to be stated next to each code where applicable.

(iv) Special instructions : Instructions for the use of 'borrowed columns'.

4. TABULATION

Tabulation is the summarisation of results in the form of statistical tables. The raw data is divided into different groups. The tabulation may be done entirely by manual methods or electronic methods. The decision as to the method of tabulation to be adopted largely depends upon various considerations such as cost, time and personnel.

When the tabulation of the data is to be done on computers, all answers must be converted into numeric form adaptable to placement on punch cards. Each respondent will be given a card and all information pertaining to him will be entered in this card. If the questionnaire is long, then two or more cards for recording each respondent's answer may be used.

In hand tabulation we may use the direct tally, the list and tally, the card sort and count methods or strip method. A short description of each method is given below.

(i) Direct Tally : If the number of respondents are small say 50 to 60 and the number of tables required are also small, direct tabulation is possible.

(ii) List and Tally Method : In this case a long sheet, double foolscape size or map drawing size is used. On the sheets, as many columns as possible are drawn. On the top of each column the code number of the question is entered. The responses are entered in the rows.

Coding Sheet

Columns								*Code*		
1	0	1	2	3	4	5	6	7	8	9
2	0	1	2	3	4	5	6	7	8	9
3	0	1	2	3	4	5	6	7	8	9
4	0	1	2	3	4	5	6	7	8	9
5	0	1	2	3	4	5	6	7	8	9

This method is easier for small surveys.

(iii) Card Sort and Count Method : In this method a thick card with columns printed on the edges is used for each questionnaire. Each column has a number. Therefore allot code number for each question/item/variable. Enter the code number of value of the response in the concerned column. Almost 40 columns can be printed on each side. Thus response for a total of 80 questions/items/variables can be entered on both sides.

This method facilitates easy sorting out. The cards pertaining to each category in a table are segregated. Then the number of cards in each category is counted and the frequency is ascertained. For sorting out the cards, chalk piece boxes can be used. The main advantage of this method is easy handling. However, if the number of items exceeds 80 this method is not useful.

Sorting Card

1	2	3	4	5	6	7
22						8
21						9
20						10
19						11
18	17	16	15	14	13	12

(iv) Strip Method : Long strip of one inch width is used in this method. Each strip has 160 columns printed on each side. Thus responses relating to 320 items can be recorded in one strip. The strip can also be folded and made easy for handling. The method of handling is the same as for cards. Strips are useful for big projects with large number of items.

(*a*) Decide the groups or class intervals.

(*b*) Write down the class intervals.

(*c*) Find out the number of items in each class interval.

(*d*) Use chalk piece box for keeping the sorted cards.

(*e*) If cards are used for transcription, sort out the cards into different groups.

4.1 METHOD OF TABULATION

Hand tabulation is simple involving no technical knowledge or skill. If the number of survey cases is small, say of the order of 100-200 or less, there may be no point in tabulating by machine. Even for small surveys if the analysis requiring complicated cross tabulation, hand tabulation willbe slow and unwieldy.

The development of electronic computers has led to tremendous advance in survey analysis. It has led to the use of high-powered multivariate statistical procedures. Most computer installations have large libraries of computer programmes and the researcher only has to discover how to use the programs of interest to him. For this purpose he does not need to know about computer languages such as Fortran, Algol and Cobol or how to write these programmes.

4.2 TYPES OF TABLES

The tables may be frequency table or response table.

Frequency Table
Textile Mills in Coimbatore Earning Profit During 1990-91

Profit (in rupees thousands)	*Number of Mills*	*Percentage*
Upto 50	5	12.5
50-100	4	10.0
100-150	8	20.0
150-200	13	32.5
200-250	7	17.5
Above 250	3	7.5
Total	40	100.00

Response Table

Response	*Number of Responses*	*Percentage*
Yes	20	40
No	30	60
Total	50	100

Dummy tables to illustrate the tabulations and comparison that will be needed, should be set up before the final research design details are settled. Data from the pilot study may be entered in these tables to indicate whether the anticipated relationship is likely to be found in the study or not.

4.3 COMPONENTS OF A TABLE

The different components of a table are :

(i) Table Number : Each table should be numbered. The number may be given either in the centre or at the top above the title.

(ii) Title of the Table : Every table must be given a suitable title. The title should be clear, brief and self explanatory.

(iii) Caption : Caption refers to column headings. It explains what the column represents. It may consist of one or more column headings. Under a column heading there may be sub-heads.

(iv) Stub : Stubs are the designations of the rows or row headings. They are at the extreme left. The stubs are usually wider than column headings.

(v) Body : The body of the table contains the numerical information. This is the most vital part of the table. Data presented in the body is arranged according to description.

(vi) Headnotes : The unit of measurement is frequently written as a headnote, such as "in thousands" or "in million tonnes" or "in crores".

(vii) Footnotes : Footnotes are used to give the sources of secondary data. They explain the heterogeneity in the data, indicate special circumstances affecting the data and clarify anything in the table.

4.4 GENERAL RULES OF TABULATION

(1) All table captions and stubs should be arranged in some systematic order.

(2) Unit of measurement must be clearly defined.

(3) Tables should not be overloaded with details.

(4) The arrangement of the table should be logical.

(5) Abbreviations should be avoided.

(6) The expression "etc" is a bad form in a table.

(7) Don't use ditto marks.

(8) If any information is not available show this fact by the letters "NA" or by dash (—).

(9) The table should suit the size of the paper.

CHAPTER ELEVEN

ANALYSIS AND INTERPRETATION OF DATA

1. *Analysis*
2. *Interpretation*

1. ANALYSIS

Analysis and Interpretation are giving meaning to the collected information by comparing them with the existing information. For example, a survey undertaken in Madras shows that the per capital income in Madras in 1984 was say Rs. 7,000/-. This information is not useful unless it can be associated with the income of the other cities.

Analysis is placing the collected data in some order or format so that the data acquire a meaning. Raw data become information only when they are placed in a meaningful form. Interpretation involves drawing conclusions from the gathered data.

1.1 PROCEDURE FOR ANALYSIS

There are three tasks to be performed if the collected data are to be used in the most effective manner.

(i) An intensive review must be made of all the data collected for the project with reference to the study's objectives and hypotheses.

(ii) These data are then analysed with the help of techniques selected earlier.

(iii) The results emerging from these anlayses are then related to the study's hypotheses and objectives.

The collected data have to be analysed fully. For example, a large detergent manufacturer made a study of market trend for his two products namely A and B. The researcher collected data regarding the sale of these two projects for the year 1990 and 1991. On the basis of the data collected, an analysis has been made. The analysis thus made is not relevant since it has not been taken into account the total bleach sales for the industry, the activities of the competitor and the causes for the decline in sales.

Some researchers make the mistake of postponing the selection of their analytical techniques until they collect the data. For example if the researcher wants to apply correlation technique to determine the degree of relationship between the two variables, he has to collect the data to perform this analysis.

It is very difficult for any one researcher to have a working knowledge of all the techniques. There are numerous articles published in various trade and academic journals describing new models and techniques for analysis. Besides, text books on statistics outline various analytical techniques. These documents should be consulted before deciding the framework of analysis.

The analysis may be descriptive analysis and casual analysis.

1.2 DESCRIPTIVE ANALYSIS

Descriptive analysis is largely the study of distribution of one variable. This analysis is in other words called one dimensional analysis. This analysis shows the benchmark data and measures the state or condition at any particular time. This analysis is the prelude to bivariate and multivariate analysis.

The management of a nationalised bank wanted to study the size of their savings account as on 31.12.1993. The frequency distribution of the Savings Bank Account is shown in the following table.

Frequency Distribution of Savings Account by Size of Account

Account Size (Rs.)	*Number of Accounts*
1 - 999	4000
1000 - 1999	3000
2000 - 2999	2000
3000 - 3999	1500
4000 - 4999	1000
5000 - 5999	500
6000 - 6999	300
7000 - and above	200

This table describes the size of Savings Bank Account of the bank as on 31.12.1983.

We can also classify certain number of accounts by occupation, residence, qualification, sex and other factors. The tables constructed based on such classification will lead to bivariate and multivariate analysis.

1.2.1 BIVARIATE ANALYSIS

The bivariate analysis is placing the collected data into tubular form so that the real meaning of these data can be derived. The starting point of Bivariate Analysis is to develop simple dimensional data. Then put the data into two or more categories. This analysis is explained with the help of a survey. A study was undertaken among Madurai City residents to determine their movie-going habits. A sample of 1,000 persons was randomly interviewed. Out of 1000 sample members 267 (26.70 per cent) are regular movie goers and 733 (73.30 per cent) are not regular movie goers. These facts are given in the following table.

Movie Attendance Among Sample Residents

Category	*Number*	*Percentage*
Regular Movie Goers	267	26.70
Not Regular Movie Goers	733	73.30
Total	1000	100.00

1.2.2 SEQUENTIAL ANALYSIS

The data presented in a table reveals one factor at a time. This analysis is called sequential analysis. A further analysis of the data regarding movie goers showed that the college students were more frequent movie goers than non-college students.

Students in Terms of Movie Attendance

Category	*College Students*	*Non-College Students*	*Total*
Regular Movie Goers	130 (37%)	137 (21%)	267
Not Regular Movie Goers	220 (63%)	513 (79%)	733
Total	350 (100%)	650 (100%)	1000

The data presented in the above table reveals one factor at the time.

1.3 CASUAL ANALYSIS

This analysis explains how one variable affects another. Some external factor products a change in the dependent variable. We may also analyse to findout whether two variables (dependent and independent) covary. There are different ways by which we might determine whether such correlations do exist or not.

A researcher is usually interested in understanding why sales are larger in some markets than in others or why some people are heavy users of a product while others do not use it at all or why some people prefer brand A while others prefer brand B.

These things (sales, consumption and preference) can be influenced or affected by product quality, advertising, price or other things which can be controlled by the manager. The variables such as sales, consumption and preference are dependent variables. Changes in brand's price, package and advertising may affect the brand's sales. These variables are called independent variables.

The cross tabulation, correlation and regression analysis are methods of analysis which can explain why there are different or variations in a dependent variable.

The statistical design of the study is based on random sampling and it enables the researcher to improve the quality of the inference.

The casual analyses are done with the help of statistical tools. For detailed discussion on various statistical analysis please refer to any standard book on 'statistics'.

2. INTERPRETATION

Interpretation means drawing inferences from the collected facts after the analytical study. According to C. William Emory interpretation has two major aspects namely establishing continuity in research through linking the results of a given study with those of another and the establishment of some relationship with the collected data.

Interpretation helps the researcher to understand the abstract principle that works beneath his findings. He can link up his findings with those of other studies having relationship with the established concept. Interpretation also enables the researcher to establish concepts, which will be the basis cf future research. Moreover, interpretation helps the target audience to understand the real significance of his research findings.

2.1 TECHNIQUES OF INTERPRETATION

Interpretation is not an easy job and it requires a great skill on the part of the investigator. The investigator gets the required expertise to apply the techniques. The techniques of interpretation are given below :

2.1.1 RELATIONSHIP BETWEEN VARIABLES

The basic object of every analytical research is to find out the relationship between any two variables. There may be three types of relationship.

Symmetrical relationship.

(ii) Reciprocal relationship.

(iii) Asymmetrical relationship.

The interpretation of data can be made with the help of these relationships.

2.1.2 PERCENTAGES

Percentages are used in making comparison between two or more series of data. They are also used to describe the relationships. The following table shows the uses of percentages.

Sales of Two Types of Cars in Tamil Nadu

Cities in Tamil Nadu	*Car X*	*Per Cent*	*Car Y*	*Per Cent*
Madras	300	30	400	20
Madurai	200	20	500	15
Coimbatore	200	20	500	25
Trichirapalli	150	15	350	17.5
Tirunelveli	150	15	450	22.5
Total	1000	100	2200	100

With the help of the above table it is easy to compare the sales of cars in different cities of Tamil Nadu.

2.1.3 AVERAGE

There are three forms of averages such as arithmetic mean, median, mode. Though there are other measures of central tendency, the above three measures are commonly used. Instead of using long statistical tables, the use of average makes the interpretation very simple.

2.1.4 DISPERSION

Dispersion refers to the amount or the magnitude of the spread. Measures of dispersion include range, inter quartile range, average deviation and standard deviation. These measures help to interpret the data more scientifically.

2.2 PRECAUTIONS IN INTERPRETATION

Correct interpretation requires a high degree of skill, care, judgement and objectivity on the part of the researcher. The following precautions have to be taken to make the interpretation purposeful.

2.2.1 ADEQUATE DATA

The data should be large and unbiased. Then only the results will represent the Universe. For example, it is reported that 25% of the lady students are married. But in a faculty only one lady student got married out of the four lady students studying in the faculty. The result does not reveal anything tangible.

2.2.2 VARIATION IN DEFINITION

Variations in definition make the comparisons inappropriate. For example, while comparing the national income firures of two countries say India and U.K., it is essential to find out whether the definition for National Incomc in both countries is the same. If the definition is different in the two countries, then the comparison is not possible.

2.2.3 ERRORS IN THE USE OF STATISTICAL TOOLS

The use of inappropriate statistical techniques, inadequate sample size and faulty calculations make the result spurious. For example, is a Chi-Square test analysis in each call single digit response shall be avoided. This is possible when large number of respondents are included for the study.

CHAPTER TWELVE

RESEARCH REPORT

1. INTRODUCTION

The final step in the research process is to make the findings available to the readers with varied interests. Some readers may be concerned only with the conclusions arrived at and they may be totally indifferent about the methodology of the study. If readers themselves are researchers, they may wish to study the techniques used in the study and the analysis made to arrive at the conclusions. Some readers may be searching for the suggestions offered for solving the problems identified by the researcher. Still some others may be interested to know the library sources of information used in the study. Therefore the researcher will give a complete and full description of his problems, his method of attacking it, his analysis and his conclusions. A careful step by step exposition of a research project will greatly help the researcher in making his own thinking clear.

2. TYPES OF REPORTS

Before the preparation of the report, the researcher has to consider the background of the potential audience, their total research situation and their technical background and knowledge. The report may be a short report or a long report.

At the beginning of the short report, there should be some brief statement concerning the authorisation of the study, the problem to be examined and its breadth and depth. Following this statement a summary should come along with the conclusions and recommendations. Short reports are appropriate for studies in which the problem is well defined. Such studies of limited scope require only limited time, personnel and money, and for it methodologies are simple and straight forward.

The long report may be a technical report or a popular report. The technical report is prepared for a specialists who are interested in understanding the technical procedure and terminology used in the research project. The report will be in technical language.

The popular report is intended for persons who have limited interest in the technical aspects of the research methodology and research findings. The audience will include laymen and even top executives who want summary reports.

When the audience comprise of both technical and non-technical people it will be necessary to develop a composite report that serves both audiences. In such situations appendices may be used to include technical data.

3. CONTENTS OF A REPORT

The mechanical format of a research report consists of three parts namely, the preliminaries, the text and the reference materials. The length of the three parts is based on the extent of the study. The following sequence is generally accepted.

(a) Title Page.

(b) Preface including acknowledgements (If desired or necessary).

(c) Table of contents.

(d) List of Tables.

(e) List of Figures or Illustrations.

The Next :

(a) Introduction.

(b) Main body of the report.

(c) Conclusion.

The Reference Material :

(*a*) Bibliography.

(*b*) Appendix or Appendices.

(*c*) Index (if any).

3.1 THE PRELIMINARIES

(a) Title Page

The following information is required to be presented in the title page.

(*i*) Title of the Thesis.

(*ii*) Designation of the Faculty (Optional).

(*iii*) Name of the Institution to which the thesis is being submitted.

(*iv*) Degree for which Thesis is presented.

(*v*) Name of the Candidate (if desired degrees may be listed after the name).

(*vi*) Month and Year in which the degree is to be granted (in some cases the date of submission of the thesis).

Specimen Title Page of a Thesis :

SMALL SCALE ENGINEERING INDUSTRY IN COIMBATORE REGION – A STUDY OF INTERRELATIONSHIP WITH LARGE SCALE INDUSTRY

by

Thanulingom. N., M.Com.

A dissertation submitted in partial fulfilment of the requirements for the degree of Doctor of Philosophy in the University of Madras

March 1982

(b) Preface

The preface (often used synonymously with foreward) may include the writer's purpose in conducting the study, a brief resume of the background, scope, purpose, general nature of the research upon which the report is being based and acknowledgement.

If the writer has little to say about his thesis that is already covered in the main body of his report, the preface may be omitted and page should be labelled 'Acknowledgements'.

Acknowledgements recognise the persons to whom the writer is indebted for guidance and assistance during the study and the credit institutions for providing funds to implement the study or for the use of personnel, facilities and other resources.

If the list of acknowledgement is short, the heading 'acknowledgements' is omitted and a brief statement containing the acknowledgement is placed slightly above the centre of the page. The word, Preface and Acknowledgements should be written in capital letters.

(c) Table of Contents

The purpose of a table of contents is to provide an analytical overview of the material included in the study or report. A specimen of the table of contents is given below :

CONTENTS

(d) List of Tables

After the Table of contents, the writer needs to prepare a list of tables. The heading, 'List of Tables' should be centred on a separate page by itself. Two spaces below this heading, appear at the left margin 'Table' and 'Page' at the right margin. The number of the table and the page number must be written in Arabic numerical. The initial letters of the key words in titles are capitalised. No terminal punctuation is used.

Specimen of List of Tables

List of Tables

(e) List of Figures

The list of figures appears in the same form as the list of tables. The page is headed List of Figures without terminal punctuation. Figures are listed at the left of the page and page at the right hand margin. Both serial number of the figure and the page number appear in Arabic numerical.

Specimen of List of Figures

List of Figures

The same procedure is followed for presenting the *List of Illustrations and List of Plates* also.

3.2 THE TEXT

The text is the most important part of a thesis. In this section the writer presents his facts or the basic tenets of his argument. The writer should devote the greater part of his energies to a careful organisation and presentation of his findings or general argument. The writer develops his thesis logically, concisely and coherently through the chapter scheme.

(a) Introduction

An introduction should be written with considerable care with two major aims – introducing the problem in a suitable context and arousing and stimulating the reader's interest. If the introduction is dull, aimless, confused and lacking precision, direction and specificity, there is little incentive for the reader to continue reading.

An introductory chapter usually contains the following :

(i) A lucid, complete and concise statement of the problem being investigated.

(ii) A description of the scope of the study.

(iii) An explanation of the need for the study and its importance.

(iv) A preview of the organisation of the thesis.

(v) A resume of the historical background and present importance of the problem.

(vi) A brief statement regarding the sources of data, the techniques used for analysing the data, the assumptions used in the analysis and the technical terminology used.

The reader reading the introductory section, will know how the data are to be handled and the purpose of the project.

(b) Main Body of the Report

The chapters constituting the main body of the report will vary in number and length according to the nature of the evidence to be presented. The arguments or findings should be presented in a logical or orderly way. Every bit of evidence should be supported by logical reasoning and empirical facts.

Materials should be organised systematically and presented under appropriate headings. Because of the diversity of research topics, it is not possible to specify directions for organising the main body of a thesis. However, the following order may be adopted.

(i) Statement of specific question or hypothesis under study.

(ii) Presentation of relevant data.

(iii) Interpretation of data.

(iv) Conclusions and interpretations for each specific question.

(c) Conclusion

The conclusion serves the important function of typing together the whole thesis. The writer may also list out unanswered questions, which require further research. If the recommendations for future action grow out of the conclusion, they should be clearly stated in the report.

3.3 THE REFERENCE MATERIAL

(a) Bibliography

The bibliography follows the main body of the text and is separate but integral part of a thesis. In compiling a bibliography the researcher may wish to subdivide primary and secondary sources; or texts and journal articles and so on. But the current practices favour a comprehensive listing. There is no division into primary sources and secondary sources or books, journals, newspapers, documents and official papers. In comprehensive listing, bibliography should follow a logical arrangement in alphabetical order.

The essential information for each book reference is the author(s), the little and details concerning the imprint.

Example :

Guildford, J.P., 1965. *Fundamental Statistics in Psychology and Education* (4th ed.), New York : McGraw Hill.

In the case of a journal the place of publication and the publisher's name are not included. But the volume number and the inclusive pages which contain the article are given.

Example:

Turner, L.C.F. 1968. The Russian Mobilisation in 1914. *Journal of Contemporary History*, 3, 65-68.

(b) Appendix

The appendix usually includes such matters as original data, tables that present supporting evidence, tests that have been constructed by the research student, parts of document or any supportive evidence that would detract from the major line of argument and would make the body of the thesis unduly large and any extract from official document. Usually the copy of the questionnaire and the interview schedule used for collecting the primary data are included in the appendix.

(c) Index

If a thesis is subsequently published as a book, monograph or bulletin, an index is necessary.

4. STEPS IN DRAFTING REPORTS

The three cardinal rules of report writing are accuracy, brevity and clarity. They are not easily mastered. It is said that hard writing makes easy reading. The report writer must constantly strive to make his reader's task as easy as the subject matter permits. A report has four stages.

4.1 PREPARATION

The researcher must first decide what information he wants to convey and how the various points are related to one another. He has to prepare a detailed outline indicating what is to be said in the thesis without worrying about how it is being said.

Once the outline is prepared the researcher has to see whether any idea is omitted and whether the ideas are grouped properly.

4.2 ARRANGEMENT OF IDEAS

Arrangements of ideas and systematic presentation will evoke the interest of the reader. The researcher has to decide the order in which he wishes to present the data. The various points can be brought out by appropriately employing centre headings, sub-headings, underling, bold face type, etc. Besides, there must be uniformity and consistency in the presentation of ideas, and punctuation, capitalisation, abbreviations, footnotes, quotations, acknowledgements and bibliography must be uniform.

4.3 WRITING

A well presented study often impresses the reader more than another study which may have greater scientific quality but a weaker presentation. The researcher should consider the following pre-writing considerations.

(i) What is the purpose of the report?

(ii) Who will read the report?

(iii) What is the gap in knowledge on the subject between the reader and the writer?

(iv) What are the circumstances and limitations under which the researcher writes his thesis?

(v) How will the report be used?

A researcher usually presents the evidence in three forms such as textual, tabular and graphical. The textual form is a running narrative of the facts in an explanatory or descriptive manner. A sincere effort should be made to minimise length so that the reading will be interesting and effective. If the data are quantitative, tables and graphs can be used.

The quantitative data can be presented in the form of tables. A table may be formal or informal. A formal table should be confined to a single page if possible. If should be numbered with Arabic numeral and must have a descriptive title. Avoid complex and unwieldy tables. The writer should assemble all the text materials relating to a given table in one spot. (An informal table is one which is integrated into text discussion without a number and title and it occupies only six or eight lines).

The graphic form appeals to the readers' visual sense and permits a ready interpretation of complicated set of relationship.

(a) Standard of Writing

Research reports are different from other academic writings. In essays the richness of words usage is often encouraged. Research reports on the other hand are designed to convey information of a more precise nature and the reporter has to choose the word more carefully and avoid ineffective communication. There should be frequent use of section and paragraph headings, numberings and listing where appropriate. Headings provide the reader with a constant reminder of where the discussion is going on. The research reporter should typically provide very wide margins on both sides as well as at the top and the bottom of the paper.

Barzun and Graff suggest some rules of thumb for overcoming inertia and achieving momentum.

(i) Don't wait until you have gathered all your materials before starting to write.

(ii) Don't be afraid of writing down something that, you think, may have to be changed.

(iii) Don't hesitate to write in any order those sections of your total work that seems to have grown ripe in your mind.

(iv) Once you start writing, keep going on. Resist the temptation to get up and verify fact. Leave it blank and afterwards fill up the blank.

(v) When you get struck in the middle of a stretch of writing, re-read your last two or three pages.

(vi) Since the right openings for chapters or sections are difficult, special attention must be paid to them.

(b) Style of Writing

(i) Let your sentences be short. The reading difficulty rests on two factors – words and relationship. Longer sentences use more words and more words cause more relationship requiring more effort by the reader.

(ii) Prefer the simple to the complex. The use of plain and simple language, short words and brief sentences is the modern and best way of writing English. If the right word is a big word,

go ahead and use it. But if a shorter word does the job, use it.

Example :

Complex Words	*Simple Words*
Utilisation	Use
Initial	First
Optimum	Best

(iii) Prefer familiar words. If the reader does not understand the words you use, his attention will go elsewhere. Therefore use familiar words.

Example :

Use 'Central Agency' instead of Nodal Agency

(iv) Avoid unnecessary words. Unnecessary words tire the reader and dull his attention.

Example :

39 Words	*17 Words*
It is the responsibility of each and every department head to properly arrange the affairs of his organisation in such a manner that each salaried employee including himself will receive the full vacation to which he is duly entitled.	Each department head must see that he and each salaried employee under him gets his full vacation.

(v) Use action words. Wordiness dilutes the vigour of any action verb. Below are few examples of diluted verbs.

Instead of this	*Try this*
Make a comment	Comment
Make a decision	Decide
are in receipt of	Received

(vi) Voices : The English language has two voices — active and passive. It requires more words to make a statement in the passive voice than it does in the active voice. The passive voice tends to slow down reading.

Example :

Active Voice – Tom writes the letter (4 words)

Passive Voice – The letter is written by Tom (6 words)

The passive voice is used in the following cases.

(i) When researcher's interest is primarily in the action performed and the person or thing receiving the action.

(ii) When the writer wants to conceal his identity e.g., It is estimated, It is proposed, etc.

(iii) Heavy connectives; Change the heavy connectives and follow more effectiveness such as then, like, because, silence, by etc.

Example :

Heavy Connective	*More Effective*
After this accomplished	then
Along the line of	like
Due to the fact that	because
In the light of the fact that	since
By means of	by

(vii) Smothered Verb: A verb is smothered when it is buried inside another word and thus loses its power to state a clear relationship.

Example :

Research resulted in the production of more economic packing (smothered verb)

Research produced more economic packing.

(viii) Punctuations : Carefully use the punctuations such as the full stop, the comma, the semi colon, the colon, the question mark, the exclamation mark, the bracket and the dash (—).

4.4 REVISION

The research report should normally go through three drafts. The objective of the first draft is comprehensiveness and fullness of facts. When the researcher has completed his first draft let him lay it aside for a day or two. Then he should criticise it objectively as if it were the work of another.

(i) Make a cursory examination of the draft. He has to examine whether the design of the report is appropriate and the heading is proper.

(ii) Check the title, table of contents, introduction and conclusion.

(iii) Examine the text in detail and weigh every statement critically.

(iv) Read the text aloud to yourself or preferably to somebody else. Does it read easily or smoothly? Can your listener follow you?

(v) Check your illustrations. Does each illustration convey its message clearly? Are the captions precise and informative?

(vi) If possible submit the draft to a person qualified to give constructive criticism.

(vii) It is often desirable to have a friend to read the draft critically and ask question which will show where greater detail or clarity is needed.

In the second draft the report should be improved both in the form and the language by considerable trimming and pruning. Ideas and sentences have to be realigned so that the report gets clarity, order, coherence and naturalness.

The final draft concentrates on the finish and the final touches on documentation to make the report authoritative and convincing.